ADHD - *Raising an Explosive child*

The Last Parents' Guide You'll Ever Need - Includes 20 Parenting Mistakes to Avoid Immediately

Oliver Miller

Table of Contents

Introduction

It has been about a decade and a half now since my sponsors, with the help of some professionals, tried their best to facilitate my gaining of access to special management strategies set aside for little children uniquely known and mostly considered to be dealing with ADHD. During these times, having to deal with a lot of stress here and there compounded by the gross misconceptions and misunderstandings, I was able to garner some intricate knowledge that has been quite profound and facilitatory to this book's making. Therein you will see the great opportunity and groundwork for achievement that nature has bestowed upon you as a parent to be a major determinant in the future of your child and the world in general.

To start, as it is often verbalized by the best specialists, knowledge is often obtained from the clients unknown to them and unaware, which are most times poorly acknowledged by these set of people touted to be the compendium of uncommon knowledge. Little do most of these specialists realize the chances of increasing their knowledge if they could only pay attention to what their patients have to say.

This was what happened to a clinician when one of his clients paid a costly visit to one of his clinic sessions on one of the busy mornings of the clinic days. The humble mother who relayed the lesson was said to be unaware of how the emotion-filled narratives of her family's situation impacted the helper she looked up to and how this later helped other families as they struggle through the woes of nature. As the clinician will later document, it was an unforgettable experience. You can also learn from what happened.

According to the clinician, the morning of this very day is what can be described as one of those mornings where everywhere is tensed and everyone is at their heels doing one thing or the other, so any element of display of niceness can be regarded as golds in the swamp. The appointment had already been scheduled, and he was to meet with a mother and her nine-year-old child, known as Smith, at 10:00 A.M., but things were not going as planned, and he had to rush into the clinic with lots of things on his mind, different charts and documents held in hand and he had to apologize for coming late on the ground of professional ethic.

He had to quickly glance through the chart to intimate himself with the demographic information that it contained, previously obtained as a routine before the appointment. After a little time doing this, he started asking some typical questions. His expectations were the usual complaints about how bad the child has been acting and how this has been affecting the family as a whole. However, he was surprised by the answers the mother gave to his questions.

As far as the clinician can tell, it is rare to hear anything different from the usual when typical questions such as "For what reason are we seeing your face today in our clinic?" is asked. Most of the time, most parents will immediately reply with various stories of how their child causes problems in school, which is always followed by other saddening and disturbing behaviors that the child exhibits when at home. Most clinicians are already adapted to hearing such responses that it is most at times assumed even before they are uttered by the parents. Some of these clinicians often, in advance, categorize the presenting complaints into school and home problems.

But that day was different; he was so surprised that morning that he claimed his mouth must have been wide opened after some moment of silence that he was induced to by the astonishment generated by the mother's responses. This is simply because his ears were surprised when they didn't hear the usual derogatory responses by mothers concerning their children's behavior and state. Responses such as "I was just told today that my child is to be suspended," "He seems to be interested in doing exactly what I tell him not to do." These were not what he heard, however. But rather, what was perceived by his sensory inlet was, "Please, I need your help. I am losing control of my child." The clinician further said he must have involuntarily asked her to repeat herself.

He said his mind wasted no time thinking what a new breed of a parent this could be. This could only be relayed by the clinician's affirmative nodding gesture in a simple show of understanding that belittled the surprise housed within his mind.

The only thing that came out of the clinician's mouth was, " I am sorry." This was later followed by "But, I don't think I understand what you are saying" to reveal his hidden internal astonishment. This kind of feeling he experienced is quite different from being simply surprised. This he called an utter surprise.

This is the main reason for the expression of lack of understanding on the clinician's part because the befitting words for such responses were yet to be documented.

What further complicated the confusion was when tears started rolling down both sides of her eyes. The mother further revealed that the ordeal had persisted for some time now, the exact time she could not remember.

"He is the last of my children," she continued, "and we are so close since he is the only boy. But I would say that he seems not to like me anymore for a long time now."

The clinician nudges her on as he couldn't rely anymore on any clinical guide for direction this time. Again the mother reiterated, "we were best of friends before all these began some years ago." The clinician had to cut in here, "how did you get to know that something had changed?" She answered, "Unlike before, he now acts cold towards me, very rebellious when I instruct him and at some times just laughs the instructions away." "In the past, we used to do several things together, which I perceived he loved, but now, he no more wants to do anything with me. He effortlessly finds an excuse to avoid me. When we communicate, he no longer looks at me the way he used to, always avoids my face, and tries to put an end to the conversation as early as he can. I just don't know what to do," exclaimed the mother.

This day was so different for the clinician; he was held back by how plain the boy's mother could express the sharp change in the relationship with her child that he had to think about his relationship with his two sons. He had to think if he is still doing well as a father. He was impressed by how the mother described the relationship between herself and the son.

He had to flash back to similar experiences with other families in the past who had visited the clinic, how he had been indifferent to their stories and narration of their family dysfunction.

This might be your story or you might have a similar story because you feel that you are losing your child all of a sudden. It happens to be that your child was just diagnosed with ADHD, and you have been working yourself out to care for the child and help the whole family to adapt, but it seems not to be working.

It might also be that you are yet to reach this stage where you can detect any changes in the way your child relates with you, but you are sure that there is something unusual about your child when compared to others of his age and urgently need someone to help out. It just seems like you have a lot of questions that you need someone to give answers to. You should know that you are not alone, whatever it may be. Presently, there are over 3 million children with ADHD. Any of the parents of these children will have similar stories to tell as well.

Raising a Child with ADHD might be difficult but not impossible.

When it comes to raising and parenting a child with ADHD, it is often very challenging for any parent. This is because these children are not attentive like other children. They are quite impulsive, overactive, and demanding. Their uniqueness can strain your role as a parent to a point you never thought of before becoming a parent. These might have even made you rethink how wise your decision to become a parent was.

When it comes to being parents for a child with ADHD, the role of parenting is somehow increased as the parents of these types of children will have to double up their activities in any areas reasonable to parenting to be able to display competency.

You will have to supervise, teach, monitor, plan, structure, reward, punish, guide, protect and nurture the child three times more than a child without ADHD to get a third of the results displayed a normal child.

They might even have to meet more often with those involved in the child's life daily. These include the child's teacher, pediatrician, and mental health professionals. There is also the daily dose of intervention with neighbors, friends, parents of friends, and others in the community made compulsory because of the greater behavioral dysfunction the child is likely to exhibit when interacting with outsiders.

The matter is further complicated by the increasing need of a child with ADHD for parental protection, support, advocacy, nurturance, and love often concealed by the cloak of excessive, unusual, and oftentimes irritating behaviors.

Most parents with a child with ADHD do find out that the task of raising a child with ADHD adds more burden to the arduous task of being a parent in the first place. The duty of a typical parent is normally filled with difficulties, and your role as a parent having a child with ADHD doubles the difficulty.

Bringing up a child with ADHD may be the hardest thing you will have to do and which you just have to be responsible for. Some parents give in to the burden such a child places on them and become distressed, resulting in constant family crisis at home and eventually leading to separation after a long time of unsuccessful attempts at resolution.

Nevertheless, you can rise to this challenge, get better at parenting your child, and give yourself the opportunity to improve as a person, get fulfilled as a parent, and even become a role model for other parents.

It is always inspiring to know that you are crucial in your child's life, and this can launch you into a deeper level of connection which may unravel other purposes to your life and reveal how you can be helpful in ways you never thought of.

However, do not think it will just happen. The health of your child is nothing to joke about. Different things will come into play. It might not even play out as you have imagined. But, you must stay focused, be committed, and let the hope of seeing your child get better be your driving force. You might not get the necessary motivation from outside, and most might be discouraging. The onus lies with you to build up your inner strength to fuel yourself to action and see your child grow to the wonderful person you have always imagined.

Chapter 1:
What is ADHD?

Since way back in 1902, the medical condition known as Attention Deficit Hyperactivity Disorder (ADHD) which some people refer to as Attention Deficit Disorder (ADD), has been given special recognition by some medical professionals.

From 1902 to 1980, ADHD was diagnosed primarily in little boys with behavior problems— they found it difficult to "sit still" and "shut up"— They exhibited behaviors that could drive anybody nuts. The name of this disorder has been changed many times; however, it's still basically about behavior problems.

It has been realized, since 1980 (when the name was first changed to include the word "attention deficit"), that this disorder is not so much a behavior problem but one that is more about the management system of the human brain—technically, it is about the executive functions of the brain. From research, it's been discovered that some individuals with ADHD never experience any significant behavior problems. For those that have experienced them, they're usually the least of it.

The Center for Disease Control and Prevention (CDC) explains ADHD as "one of the most common neurodevelopmental disorders of childhood. It is usually diagnosed in childhood and often lasts into adulthood." Attention Deficit Hyperactivity Disorder in children can be identified when they develop challenges with managing behaviors such as impulsiveness (acting with no thought about the consequence), inattentiveness, or hyperactivity.

American Psychiatric Association (APA) shows that ADHD as a mental disorder can also affect many adults. Adults with ADHD may experience the same symptoms as that of the children: hyperactivity (an inordinate movement that isn't fitting to the setting), inattention (experiencing trouble to keep focus), and impulsivity. APA shows the estimate of 2.5% of adults and 8.4% of children battling with ADHD.

Thomas E. Brown, Ph.D., Associate Director at the Yale Clinic for Attention and Related Disorders, expressed that ADHD does not have anything to do with how smart someone is. He claimed to have treated different individuals with ADHD, some university professors, doctors, lawyers, big business owners, and even regular people. These are smart people, right? Yes, but some of them still have problems doing the basics. So, being smart does not mean you can't develop this condition. The fact is that you can fall within anywhere along the IQ spectrum and still have ADHD.

Attention Deficit Hyperactivity Disorder (ADHD) is a set of problems that contains a wide range of characteristics. ADHD involves many important things. One of the essential things to know is that people experiencing ADHD tend to complain about the challenge they face as far as trying to stay attentive is concerned. People with ADHD tend to lose concentration from time to time, usually when reading, listening, or working on something. They find it difficult to maintain a hundred percent of focused attention.

Moreover, people with ADHD face the challenge of regular distraction. Like everyone else, they can hear and see things around them and have thoughts going through their heads. As it may be easy for many people to push things that distract them out of their minds and focus on what they need to do, it is not for people with ADHD. They tend to lose focus and concentration as their minds wander away from a specifics task to something else.

Thomas E. Brown analogically presents a situation where people with ADHD sit in the classroom with the primary intention to listen attentively or focus on what they are reading or writing, but a distraction occurs, which may be the dropping of a pencil by someone. Brown said what they will do will be to check and see in what direction the pencil goes. After returning to their initial position, to continue their task, they will focus for some minutes but get lost in thought again, thinking about the TV show they saw, then back again to the task, and then lost in thought again. This can repeat itself again and again as many times as possible.

Moreover, Thomas E. Brown claims that it may sometimes be difficult to understand people with ADHD because several individuals with this disorder have what they can do and, incredibly, they have no issue with paying proper attention or staying focused while doing it.

Thomas cites the case of a very smart teenage boy who is always in trouble with his teacher, even though he's amazing when it comes to being a goalie. The challenge he has is with concentration and focus, but they, the teachers, are amazed he can concentrate for long periods when playing hockey. They presume if he can do that, he should be able to do the same in class.

Another good example Thomas gives is about a kid whose teacher complains that she can't concentrate for more than 5 minutes. This assertion is debunked because they have seen her level of concentration when she sits to play video games; she can play for hours without remembering to even eat. So, if she can concentrate like this, why can't she do the same in school?

According to him, there are several people with ADHD that have a few things they can do with no trouble paying attention, even though on almost everything else, they have a lot of trouble paying attention. Moreover, if you ask someone with ADHD some questions like "What's with this? How come you can do it here, and you can't do it there?" The usual response they will give is, "It's easy. If it's something I'm interested in, I can pay attention. If not, I can't." Most people that hear this kind of response may answer with, "yeah, right. Congratulations." That's true for almost everybody, if not everybody. We tend to pay better attention to activities we are passionate about than those we are not interested in.

However, there is a clear difference. Thomas shows that people without ADHD can concentrate on something if they know that it must be done. But for those with ADHD, it's difficult unless they personally find the task enjoyable; someone telling them a task is interesting doesn't count.

So, there won't be any problem if this condition is met— their focus can be guaranteed. If not, it becomes really difficult for them to focus. Where the real issue lies is that it's not a condition that is under voluntary control. People may sometimes see it as a problem with willpower. Nonetheless, it's never a problem with willpower. It's a problem with the way their brain is wired.

According to Thomas, some things constitute the range of difficulties that people with ADHD complain about. Some of these include problems with memory, difficulty controlling their actions, regulating emotions, regulating alertness and sleep, focusing and shifting focus when the need arises.

It's important to know that all the characteristics of ADHD are problems that everybody does experience sometimes. Nonetheless, people with Attention Deficit Disorder tend to have "a lot more difficulty with it more of the time."

People with ADHD:

- Often have trouble getting organized and getting started on things.
- Often experience a lot of difficulties regulating their sleep and their alertness and keeping up the effort to finish things in a reasonable time.
- Have trouble staying with a task. They may be a good starter, starting the specific task reasonably well, but they have

difficulty keeping up the effort to finish it in a reasonable time. Yes, everybody has a problem with deadlines sometimes. For people with ADHD, it's almost like they can't complete a task until it becomes a pressing issue.

- Often have trouble in writing. Here, the issue is not with penmanship at all. It's bringing up ideas and constructively organizing them into sentences and paragraphs. People with ADHD experience difficulty organizing thoughts and expressing them through words in a reasonable way.

- Often complain about difficulty managing their emotions. Although this is not one of the official criteria for Attention Deficit Hyperactivity Disorder (ADHD), many people with ADHD are concerned about it.

- Often experience problems with their working memory. It's important to know that these people tend to have an adept log-term memory. They usually don't have a problem remembering something that has happened in the past (a long time ago), but for what happened just a few minutes ago or yesterday, often they can't tell you.

- Also often have problems managing their actions. A lot of them may have challenges with "slowing down when they need and speeding up when they need to." On most occasions, they tend to have difficulty in monitoring how they act. They may speak out of turn sometimes and ignore taking into account what the effects of such an action may be. They may also jump headlong into something without giving the question, "what's going to happen if I do this?" a deep thought.

ADHD is a serious condition that requires special medical attention. People with this disorder have a lot more trouble with the aforementioned things that can be seen in them. Therefore, according to Thomas, what should be taken into account is not if it happens but how it interferes with your child's day-to-day livelihood.

Chapter 2:
How to recognize ADHD symptoms in children

It might be somehow tedious to identify symptoms specific for children with Attention Deficit Hypersensitivity Disorder (ADHD). This can be partly attributed to the fact that presenting symptoms that are identifiable among children can also be seen in adults.

Most times, parents do conclude abruptly that all of their children do exhibit symptoms of ADHD. Therefore, it becomes imperative to state before the proper description of the identifiable symptoms that these behaviors are typically normal compared with other normal childhood behaviors. Symptoms of ADHD are better understood in light of their patterns, intensity, and persistency.

However, keep in mind that the symptoms discussed in this chapter are by no means a tool for making a diagnosis. But, it can be used as a tool for screening to determine whether the behavior of a child will need a specialist evaluation or not.

It is only the specialist that can determine whether a child's symptom is severe compared to others of his age group, whether the pattern of symptoms is in line with that of ADHD, and decide if it is truly ADHD. This is because the specialist is properly trained, certified, and licensed to diagnose such a condition. He/she has also gathered the necessary clinical experience to be able to do so.

If you suspect in any way that your child is exhibiting some of the symptoms that will be outlined in this chapter, such as restlessness, distractibility, poor coordination, and high demandingness, it is advised that you seek the services of a licensed, certified, and competent specialist who will help out with the right diagnosis and the suitable course of action.

Lastly, it should be noted that the identified symptoms presented in this chapter are in no way exhaustive. These symptoms might be present in some children but not necessarily found in all children diagnosed with ADHD. Also, it has been found that ADHD is typically three times more common in boys than girls.

Low level of attention and high level of distraction

One prominent symptom common to children with ADHD is their high level of distraction and short attention span.

When it comes to children with ADHD, they cannot place their attention on a specific element or object for a long period. Compared to adults, young children normally do not have a long attention span and cannot follow through on lengthy and difficult tasks. An ADHD child behaves like a younger child than himself.

He is quite the opposite of someone who will sit patiently in a corner and rack his brain to crack a puzzle having no space for any interruption. If he is a nursery school pupil or a toddler, he will be moving from one activity to another, unstable, and unable to focus his attention on any one activity. His teachers at school will be quite frustrated with his inability to follow instructions.

Even though most times an ADHD child only exhibits behavioral problems that have to do with his attention and increased distractibility at school, these symptoms can also be observed at home when he is interacting with his friends in the neighborhood. The child might show his reduced attention span by interrupting a story narration by one of his friends all of a sudden because he missed a point of the story. As this persists, he is tagged as being dull or weird by his mates.

Similarly, the child may simply forget the guiding instructions for a game and get discouraged later on with his continuous mistakes despite several attempts at winning the game just because he didn't pay enough attention to the instructions. This is why some sports coaches demand that ADHD members of the team take their medication before the beginning of the game.

In the house, the mother will notice that he cannot school himself to listen for long periods. It might just be that the child was told to eat with the fork and not with his hands; immediately, he complies, but after a few seconds, he goes back to eating with his hands. He might also start his assignments as instructed but fail to complete them unless his parents nag him. It is not that he intentionally disobeys instructions given; it's just that he has moved on to another activity in the middle of the assignment. When he is given a task, they are left half done. When he tries to arrange his room, it is left uncompleted. In some instances, he appears to remember but gets reluctant to comply, while in some other times, it is just that he is distracted from the present task and forgets he had one in the first place.

It should be noted that it is not all the time a child with ADHD will be distracted. In most cases, he performs better when he is constantly monitored regularly and independently. This might lead to the teacher reporting that "he fares better with a one-to-one close monitoring."

He is hyperactive

Not all ADHD children exhibit hyperactivity. Nonetheless, most of them are very active. And hyperactivity as behavior is something that you can not miss. Most children with ADHD have been active since infancy. Parents of these children have always reported that their children have been quite different from their peers from the very beginning.

Most times, these children are pretty restless, have issues with their feeding process (often filled with moments of successive and incomprehensible crying). Also, they find it difficult to sleep. Some find it difficult to initiate sleep which makes them sleep late; some wake up frequently or too early, while others fall into a deep sleep and are difficult to rouse.

As these infants grow up, most of them discover more energy; from where? I have no idea. There are frequent reports from ADHD children's parents that after having to deal with their hyperactivity and restlessness of their infants, they tend to learn how to walk at a very early age, and like a mini hurricane, match forth, destroying every obstacle in their way.

One of the parents, when narrating her ordeal, said that her kid is always on the move, always tampering with everything in the house, always touching one object or the other, and usually breaks objects. When she takes her eyes off him for just a minute, the kid often somehow climbs up the refrigerator or may just be found walking into the middle of the street. Within the twinkle of an eye, he might just stumble into the kitchen and wreck anything along his path and, if luck is not on his side, hurt himself in the process. The kettle and the lamps are not left behind in the wake of this destruction. She thinks that to take her eyes off her kid is just like one paying a paid trip to the city of disaster. That moment she takes her eyes away from the kid is enough to cause untold damages in the house and put the young kid's life in danger.

She might just be right because ADHD children are more often than not casualties of accidents and have more potential to be seen in emergency sections of the hospital than non-ADHD children. Just don't let him obtain that driver's license, or you are sure to have an automobile accident case to deal with.

As an ADHD child gets on in years, the story changes; he is now uncontrollably on the move, always in motion as if driven by an inexhaustible motor, constantly fidgeting, drumming his fingers, shuffling his feet.

One important thing that needs to be noted is that not all ADHD children are hyperactive, some have many of the symptoms that have been discussed so far but are not overactive at all, and there are even some who are even less than normally active. This is possible if these children have been trained to be quiet to avoid being embarrassed.

Nevertheless, many other symptoms like short attention span, vulnerability to distraction, and poor organization can manifest without signs of hyperactivity.

Also, the first of the symptoms that will disappear as the child matures is the well-defined hyperactivity behavior. It might persist in passive states in some cases. An ADHD adolescent or adult might continue to fidget or shuffle the feet and might perceive himself to be very restless, unable to sit still for long, and have an affinity for energetic activities and extreme sports.

In most cases, there is always a persisting symptom. These persisting symptoms require due management, despite the overactivity getting resolved.

ADHD children are impulsive

Another symptom that is frequently seen with ADHD children is impulsivity, or the inability to properly control their impulses. Every young child wants to have what he wants whenever he wants it.

He does act without thinking or considering the consequences. The propensity to cope with delays, to wait for a while before acting is not a common trait for children, especially those with ADHD. A child without ADHD can usually listen to reason and stop asking. But that never happens with your child; no matter what you say or how you say it, he still wants what he asked for.

An ADHD child reacts angrily and spontaneously to upsetting situations or people when he feels they are behaving contrary to how he wants them to do. Toys might be kicked or broken sometimes if not behaving as expected; friends and siblings might get soaked or injured if they fail to meet his demands.

When a child is impulsive, you get to know by the disorganized planning and poor decision-making. Though it is quite difficult to spell out how much good planning and judgment are expected from a child, nonetheless, an ADHD child will perform poorly in this area when compared to age-appropriate behaviors. ADHD children tend to be severely off in different ways. They are often very disorganized and disorderly. Their poor control of impulses aggravates their distractibility resulting in disorganized rooms, unfinished assignments, disordered reading, and uncontrolled writing.

Again, it should be noted that just like hyperactivity often goes unnoticed, impulsivity does too. It might just be that the child is just inattentive. This is because hyperactivity and impulsivity might be overlooked as being normal with children, but inattention might not be considered as such.

Their behavior is attention-demanding

An ADHD child seeks attention from others, but this is not what makes him different from others in itself. He is not the same as others and difficult to deal with simply because of his insatiability. Just like a young child, he desires to be at the center of attention. To achieve this, he might whine, tease, cry and act in ways to get you irritated without stopping. This manifestation gradually changes as he grows up.

Being a toddler, he might act out those annoying behaviors and be disobedient to instructions that he had complied with earlier. As he grows older, he may try to direct discussions on the dinner table towards himself or be a clown at school or show off to his friends, either by having expensive items or putting himself in dangerous situations. The desire to be at the center of attention can be so distressing, annoying, and confusing to the parents.

The symptoms highlighted here, as stated earlier, are by no means exhaustive. They are the frequently observed symptoms among ADHD children.

Chapter 3:
Causes of ADHD

What Causes ADHD?

You might have gone through a gazillion questions in your mind. Questions to which you desire answers. Questions such as "Why is this happening to my child? Where did I go wrong? What is the reason for this? Am I responsible for this? What is going on?" This line of questioning will only lead to self-blame, which will be of no help to you or your child because you most likely didn't cause your child's disorder.

Since the discovery of the ADHD condition, diverse studies have been carried out. These studies have continued to step further into analyzing what might be responsible for this condition.

However, there is a shortage of research evidence that is compelling enough to show that ADHD can be directly a product of faulty social methods or poor child-rearing method

More of what can be proved seems to stem from the area of neurobiology and genetics. This is in no way stating that environmental factors are not in one way or another contributory to the development and severity of this condition, especially the extent of the disability, dysfunctioning, and suffering that an ADHD child experiences. It is just that current evidence does not yet prove that such factors can directly result in ADHD all by themselves.

It is very important to state that the parents' focus should be on looking ahead and searching for the best and most suitable ways of getting the needed help for their children.

The main aim of scientists studying the causes of ADHD is to find a better way of managing the condition and, if possible, get ways to prevent its development. After a series of studies and searching, more and more evidence is being discovered, creating an image of the fact that ADHD is not a direct result of the way things are in the home. I hope this knowledge relieves you of the guilt you have been driving yourself insane with. Your style of parenting is not the cause!

For the last few years now, some new theories have been discovered by scientists about what might be the causes of ADHD. Though some of these theories have led to dead ends, others have created exciting new avenues that can be investigated.

Different environmental agents

Several studies have been carried out to show the possible correlative relationship between drug usage and alcohol intake during pregnancy and the chances of the fetus developing ADHD within the uterus. Therefore, as a precaution, it is advised that pregnant women desist from cigarette use and alcohol intake during pregnancy.

Another agent present in the environment that might contribute to higher vulnerabilities to ADHD development is the presence of high levels of lead in the body's system of young preschoolers. That is one of the main reasons why lead is no longer permitted as a component in the production of paints. For this reason, lead can rarely be found in new buildings, so the risk of exposure to toxic levels of lead is not as prevalent as it was in the past, although the same can't be said about all old buildings. Children who still live in old buildings where lead is present in the plumbing or in the paint used to conceal them may be at risk.

Brain injuries

There was a theory in the early years of studies on causes of ADHD which states that the condition can be attributed to sustained injury to the brain. According to this theory, children who have been victims of accidents that lead to injuries to the brain may display some behavioral signs similar to those of ADHD. Though only a small percentage of identified children diagnosed with ADHD have been found to have been victims of traumatic brain injuries in the past.

Sugars and food additives

It has also been a popular suggestion that attention disorders can be attributed to the intake of refined sugars and food additives. It is also believed that symptoms of ADHD are aggravated by the intake of sugars or food additives.

There was a scientific consensus organized by the National Institutes of Health in 1982 to discuss this issue. During the conference, it was discovered that diet restrictions helped an estimate of 5 percent of children with ADHD disorder, who are mostly young children with food allergies.

There was another recent study on the effect of the consumption of sugars in children. In the study, the use of sugars and a substitute on alternate days was employed, with the parents, staff, and children kept in the dark concerning the type of substance used. The study's findings showed that there is no significant effect of sugar on the behavior of the children and their learning process.

Further study was carried out to clarify the opinion of mothers who felt that their children are sugar sensitive. Their children were administered aspartame to serve as a substitute for sugar. Unlike the previous study, where all the parents were ignorant of the substance used for testing, half of the mothers were informed that their children were given sugar while the other half were told that aspartame was given to their children. Those mothers who had the foreknowledge that their children were given sugar opined that their children were more hyperactive than others.

Brain Chemistry

A certain number of scientists have hypothesized that some specified group of neurotransmitters are not in the right quantity in children with ADHD when compared to those that are without the condition. These neurotransmitters are chemicals inside the brain tissues that allow the transmission of information from one nerve to another. Some other findings have also supported this suggestion. These include:

1. Some stimulating drugs called stimulants and their non-stimulant counterpart, reputed for modifying the neurotransmitters, improve the behavior of those diagnosed with ADHD at least for a short while.

2. Certain research involving animals has also discovered that these types of drugs tend to simulate the production of some neurotransmitters. A good example is the typical dopamine and norepinephrine neurotransmitters inside the brain. It was discovered that these stimulants and non-stimulants generate a good number of positive improvements in the behavior of children with ADHD. This shows that these drugs are causing an increase in the quantity of these two chemicals produced within the brain, which means that these two chemicals are expected to be produced in smaller quantities within those with ADHD.

3. When those neurotransmitter pathways located inside the brain, which are rich with these identified neurotransmitters such as dopamine, are selectively damaged by a specific chemical in tested young animals, for example, rats and dogs, they become very hyperactive as they grow older. Studies such as this have also discovered that this kind of hyperactivity can be lowered by the administration of stimulants, the same kind of drugs helpful in managing children with ADHD.

4. Also, some research carried out involved obtaining some samples of spinal fluids from children with ADHD to investigate if they contained a similar quantity of certain chemicals also produced within the brain. These sets of research have helped identify the possibility that a reduction in the number of certain neurotransmitters such as dopamine may contribute to the development of ADHD. Though reports from other studies where quantities of such neurotransmitters were assayed using urine and blood samples have often been in disagreement with this line of conviction.

Genetics

Not quite long ago, some scientists carried out hundreds of research using various strategies to identify some genes that might be involved in the development of ADHD. As of now, at least about four genes have been identified to be associated with ADHD development.

Other genes were also identified that affect brain growth, nerve cell migration during development, and connections between nerve cells. Children with ADHD have been discovered to have dissimilar versions of these genes that affect the identified neurotransmitters compared to those without the condition.

There has also been evidence that shows that ADHD can be inherited across family generations. This implies that there is a likelihood that the body's genes are influential in its development. Studies have shown about 25 percent of very intimate relatives within the family of ADHD patients are born with the markers of this condition. The rate is much lower in the general population and is considered to be about 5 percent.

There continue to be several other studies by researchers into the contribution of the genes to the development of ADHD and to identify the specific genes that are making people susceptible to the development of ADHD.

Since its creation in 1999, the Attention Deficit Hyperactivity Disorder Molecular Genetics Network has served as an avenue through which researchers across the world can share their findings of the possible contribution of the body genetic makeup to the development of ADHD disorder.

What recent studies are saying on the causes of ADHD

Having a fair knowledge about the brain's anatomical structure and the corresponding functioning of each part can help understand what the research scientists are doing when they try to look for physical determinants for attention deficit hyperactivity disorder (ADHD).

A major part of the brain that has been the main focus for research scientists so far is the cerebral frontal lobes. The frontal lobes are the site responsible for critical thinking, problem-solving, planning, the ability to comprehend the behavior of those around you, and controlling and refraining yourself from being too impulsive. There are two frontal lobes known as the right and the left frontal lobes. These two lobes communicate and interact with each other via the corpus callosum, which are nerve fibers that bridge and connect the right and left frontal lobes.

The basal ganglia are the interconnected gray masses located deep within the cerebral hemisphere, which serve as the linkage between the cerebral and the cerebellum. These regions are responsible for motor coordination.

Most of these parts of the brain are being studied via different methods for investigating or looking into the brain. Examples of the different methodologies include the MRI known as Magnetic Resonance Imaging and the improved versions of the computed tomography scan. With the help of these methods, the actual and implied psychological dysfunction associated with individuals with ADHD is being rigorously investigated.

The Psychiatry Branch of children of the National Institute for Mental Health (NIMH) early in this decade studied more than 150 boys and girls diagnosed with ADHD and matched them with a control group consisting of more than 130 boys and girls of similar age without ADHD. These children were assessed at least twice, some of them as much as four times for up to a decade. Being the group that was given the intervention, children with ADHD were observed to have some percentage decrease in the size of the brain in the regions that were evaluated from the fore region of the brain to the hind part and the deepest portion.

The study also revealed that children with ADHD who were given medications were discovered to experience a reduction in the size of the white matter to a number similar to that of those in the control groups. This part of the brain, known as "white matter," is made up of fibers that can establish connections capable of traveling across long distances between regions in the brain. It is expected to thicken normally as the child increase in age, and there is a corresponding maturity of the brain.

Even though this particular study which is long-term in design, made use of Magnetic Resonance Imaging (MRI) for the scanning of the Children's brains, the research scientist emphasized that this investigative procedure is only yet a research tool and has not yet been approved for diagnosis of ADHD in any child. This also goes for other neurological methodologies that are used for assessing the normal functioning of the brain.

Chapter 4:
ADHD and Anxiety

When it comes to children with ADHD, anxiety is something that cannot be done away with. About 50% of children with ADHD develop anxiety. This is because these children face many challenges too early in life. These challenges can make these children become quite anxious and make them more vulnerable to anxiety than other kids of their age, or they may have inherited the anxiety gene.

It can be hard to tell whether a child has ADHD or anxiety because there's so much overlap in how their symptoms appear. Here's what you need to know about ADHD and anxiety — and what you can do to help your child.

Sometimes, it is difficult to differentiate whether a child has ADHD or anxiety because there are many similarities in how these two conditions manifest among the kids.

ADHD-Anxiety connection

Children who have ADHD do have difficulties with their executing skills. These are the skills needed for the organization, planning, time management, and normal day-to-day activities. Having to struggle with these skills daily can be quite discouraging and distressing. The persistence of this can lead to the development of anxiety.

Children who have ADHD find it more difficult to deal with stress. This is because ADHD influences how effectively a child can manage his emotions; they either feel everything or nothing at all. ADHD children may become too emotional to think clearly about how to deal with distressing situations.

Therefore, the presence of ADHD can result in the development of anxiety. Also, children with ADHD are three times more vulnerable to developing anxiety than other children. This is because ADHD and anxiety often develop concurrently.

How an anxious child who has ADHD may behave

Emotions that develop due to attempts to manage distressing and troublesome situations may affect a child's behavior in several ways. In some children, there is an unusual calmness and withdrawal from others, while some other children try to flare up and attract attention to themselves.

Below are some behaviors that may be signs that a child with ADHD has anxiety:

- Act excessively like a clown in the class

- Always become easily angered and very argumentative

- Tell all kinds of lies and give excuses about given assignments and other assigned responsibilities that were not done

- Gradually withdraw from all social activity which may be in the form of locking himself in his bedroom or bathroom

- Spends an exuberant amount of time on video games and TV

Reasons why anxiety is sometimes misdiagnosed as ADHD

In some cases, children with anxiety may be misdiagnosed with ADHD and vice versa. This is because taking a surface look, both conditions have similarities in their manifestations. Below are some of the ways children with either condition may behave but for different motives.

Finding it difficult to focus his attention: Children with anxiety may seem engaged or preoccupied, but in reality, they are just locked in their minds, thinking of worst-case scenarios. Children with ADHD lose their focus and attention because of some modifications in the brain, affecting regions that control focus.

Always fidgeting: Anxious children may continue to tap their feet incessantly during classes because of their nervousness. ADHD children do fidget because of the high level of activity called hyperactivity and impaired impulse control.

Slow with work: Anxious children are often slow when working because of the internal desire to do their assigned jobs without any mistake. ADHD children tend to take their time when they get things done because of the difficulty in starting a task and focusing on it.

Fails to achieve given assignment: Anxious children often find it difficult to find their way around a given assignment because they are too anxious to think or ask for help. Children with ADHD have issues with their assignments because of the high level of forgetfulness and low planning skills.

Find it difficult to initiate friendship: Socially anxious children are often afraid of making friends in social situations. Children with ADHD may have issues trying to interpret a social cue because of a shortage in attention span. Also, their impairment in controlling their impulse may irritate or detract other children.

Several more symptoms look very much alike between anxiety and ADHD, but there are also specific differences you can look out for. Below are some of them:

Anxious children often strive to achieve perfectionism.

Children with ADHD often find it difficult to organize their things. This is not so common among anxious children.

Anxious children often disturb themselves more about the problems they have with socializing than those with ADHD.

Children with severe anxiety disorders suffer from panic attacks when in a situation that aggravates their panic.

What you can do to help

You should be ready to identify the signs of anxiety in your child and note what you observe. You can make use of an anxiety tracker to be able to understand better when and why your child is feeling anxious.

This is another thing that you can do

You can try to understand your child's behavior: It is advised that you stop scaring them and ask how you can help. You should know that whenever they are acting up or retreating to games and TV, it may be that that they are quite anxious. You should try to find out what is responsible for their uneasiness and anxiety.

When your child is talking about his anxiety, try and empathize with those feelings and work together with them to figure out the next steps to take.

Be conscious of your anxiety: A good number of parents of anxious children also struggle with anxiety. You need to understand that your child is gradually learning how to react to distressing situations by looking at how you react to them. Children often find it easy to develop good coping skills by watching their parents cope with their stresses.

Avoid taking things personally: It can indeed be quite infuriating when your child returns from school only to give you attitude and just be plain disrespectful. You need to understand that that is one of the ways these children let out the pent-up steam within them after having a stressful day. When you observe that things are calm, you should inquire from your child the source of such tension and brainstorm ways to safely and respectfully let them out when next he feels that way to avoid hurting your or anyone else's feelings.

Direct your child towards the main objective: For example, your child might just burst into flames after a mathematics assignment. You need to calm down and wait for his high emotions to die down. Thereafter, you encourage the child to reflect on what was responsible for the feelings. Then agree together on what both of you can do the next time such occur to calm down the anxiety.

Think about getting external help: In case you have been observing that the anxiety of your child is getting in the way of his normal functioning and way of life, you should talk to your health care provider. If necessary, they will refer you to a mental health professional who will assist your child, and you find a suitable way of management.

You need to know that it is important to get a deep evaluation of your child's condition to ascertain the presence of ADHD or anxiety disorder, or both. This is very necessary when you are thinking about getting him some medications. This is because ADHD medication may help out with anxiety in some children but may also complicate matters in others. It all depends on the individual variations.

In reality, anxiety might persist for some children with ADHD. It is also essential to know that the mind can be adequately managed with the right support at home and in school.

Chapter 5:
ADHD and Sleep

ADHD is a condition that starts in childhood and comprises different symptoms, as stated earlier, including inattention, hyperactivity, and impulsivity. These identified symptoms do meddle with normal functioning in the school, homes, and also during social situations. This condition can be seen in a good percentage of the younger population, and it is more common among male children. For most of those affected, the condition does progress into adulthood due to a lack of adequate and suitable management though the quality of life of those affected can be improved if the necessary and correct management is accessed.

A 2008 study has shown that about 70 % of children diagnosed with ADHD have trouble falling and staying asleep, and in adults, 78% have a delayed circadian rhythm; this is alarming because it happens in just 20% of the general public without ADHD. Recently, steps have been taken to facilitate proper understanding of the connections between ADHD and problems with sleeping, the importance of treating these problems, and the possible contribution this can make to alleviate ADHD symptoms and the quality of life of ADHD patients and their families.

Is there any connection between ADHD and sleep?

Starting from when puberty comes knocking, people with ADHD have a higher tendency to experience reduced sleeping time, more difficulty falling asleep and remaining asleep, and a higher chance of developing a sleep disorder.

Another thing that is also common among children diagnosed with ADHD is nightmares, especially those children with difficulty sleeping. Difficulty in sleeping among children with ADHD tends to worsen as they progress in age. It has also been discovered that sleeping problems during childhood are risk factors that might develop into ADHD symptoms in the future.

Restless sleep or inadequate sleep patterns makes the brain resort to hyperactivity to keep itself awake during the day. So some children who were not that active during the day might just be victims of racing thoughts and become a reservoir of excess energy at night. Others hold on to this energy and put it to use at night because nighttime is a perfect time to concentrate and focus this energy on a particular task because there are fewer distractions.

Nonetheless, this energetic condition is quite disadvantageous for sleep initiation and can cause a disruption in the normal regulation of the sleep-wake cycle, which will over time worsen the situation and lead to the development of stressful emotion whenever it is time to initiate sleep.

Several others with ADHD find that they start sleeping during the daytime suddenly and find it difficult to wake up because of poor sleep during the night, disrupting their day. Several others experience restlessness, disturbed sleep, which is filled with several episodes of nighttime awakening.

Problems with sleeping among those with ADHD seem to differ from person to person. There are those individuals who have issues with focusing their attention for a long time. Such people have more tendency to sleep very late, while those whose predominant symptom is the combination of hyperactivity and impaired impulse control have a higher likelihood of suffering from difficulty initiating sleep.

Those who are dealing with the complexity of hyperactivity, impaired impulse control, and shortage of attention span altogether do have issues initiating sleep very early, and after successfully falling asleep, they experience poor sleep quality riddled with moments of waking up during the night hours.

Taking a critical analysis of some of the symptoms of ADHD shows that they are quite similar to symptoms of sleep deprivation. Among others, sleeping issues associated with ADHD include increased forgetfulness and difficulty focusing on a task for a long time. For children with ADHD, there might be the issue of increased tiredness which is a result of hyperactivity and impulsivity.

At certain periods, it can be very difficult to say these issues are particularly caused by ADHD or lack of sleep, or poor sleep quality. This often leads to misdiagnosis and may cause sleeping problems to go unnoticed or untreated. This has made experts recommend screening of people for sleeping problems before the administration of ADHD medication.

What is the theory behind the ADHD and Sleep connection?

Sleeping problems among ADHD children might be a side effect of the poor or difficult awakening process from sleep, alertness, and issues with the regulating circuits in the brain. Many other researchers have hypothesized that sleeping problems present in those with ADHD can be traced to the dysfunctional circadian rhythm with a delayed onset of melatonin production.

Taking into consideration the similarities between certain sleep disorders and symptoms seen among those with ADHD has led to different researches to know out if everyone with ADHD has sleep problems. But, these researches have not been able to find any consistency with abnormalities associated with sleeping among people with ADHD.

Some of these people have no issues falling asleep because of the calming effects of the stimulant medication that is widely prescribed for those with ADHD. But, for several others, these medications are counterproductive and are responsible for the diverse sleeping problems. Other co-existing disorders, such as anxiety, depression, or substance abuse, and poor sleep hygiene, are also likely contributory to the development of difficulties associated with sleep.

In what ways do sleeping problems affect the daily activities of those with ADHD?

Even though there is no sufficient data to be able to make an informed decision on the subject of ADHD and the possible accompanying sleeping problems, children and adolescents who are diagnosed with ADHD and are also having issues with sleeping do report that their symptoms are a little more severe when compared to others who have reported to sleep fine and also experience poor quality of life. Also, they are likely to deal with other conditions such as depression, anxiety, hyperactivity, lack of attention, and difficulty in comprehending difficult situations. In the long run, sleeping problems that persist leaves a child with ADHD vulnerable to other health problems.

Sleeping during the day can seriously impact school activities and performance at work. This may lead to others finding it difficult to understand why those with ADHD sleep at inappropriate times without knowing that these behaviors are just part of what the condition predisposes those who are dealing with it to and are quite difficult to avoid. Uncontrollable bouts of sleepiness can also be dangerous while driving or performing other activities that demand being focused and concentrating.

Difficulty sleeping well at night can also be responsible for fatigue during the day. Those who have ADHD-related sleep deprivation problems may feel grumpy, quite irritable, restless, tired, or have trouble paying attention at school or work.

Which type of sleeping problems are common with those with ADHD?

People who are diagnosed with ADHD are reported to have higher than normal rates of some specified sleep problems in addition to generalized insomnia. Because ADHD symptoms do resemble the symptoms of these sleep problems, underlying sleeping disorders often go unnoticed. Some children with ADHD have difficulties communicating how they are feeling, which has led to a lot of misdiagnoses of ADHD when in the actual sense, their problems are because of a sleep disorder or the combination of both ADHD and sleep disorder.

Chapter 6:
ADHD and Anger

You might have seen a child with ADHD get angry, and you were disturbed with the thoughts of whether both conditions are related. As you continue to read, you will learn that flared-up tempers are quite common among children with ADHD.

Children with ADHD are often faced with distressing situations. These children can be highly sensitive but may also find it difficult to express themselves easily. This is why they might feel bad when they let out some outburst of anger long after you have forgotten about it.

Below are some of the reasons children with ADHD may have anger issues and how you can be of help.

Built-up stress and ADHD

Some children with ADHD have a negative experience during school hours that their family members are ignorant of. You can imagine their day going like this:

The child arrives at school without doing his homework which he has to submit, and the teacher is interested in knowing why this is so. Later, the child cannot even remember the direction for the exercise, so there is no way he can finish it. During lunch, he is teased by the other children and is later called to the front of the class for distracting one of his classmates.

Then, boom, time to go home and face more tasks, which means more things may still go wrong. Remember, it has already been a stressful day for the young child, but as a parent, you are not aware of this, so you request he go and make his bed that he refused to make in the morning, which causes the already stressed child to burst out in anger.

ADHD and trouble controlling the self

Among the main highlights of ADHD is impulsivity, which makes a child speak without taking a moment to analyze his thought, and he may not even be feeling angered.

Imagine if the impulsivity is compounded by anger, you shouldn't expect anything but an explosion. While other children without ADHD might try to control themselves as they want to explode, children with ADHD do not have such control. They might either slam the door or kick the furniture.

Trying to control one's anger involves some skills that can be quite difficult for children with ADHD. First on the list is that the emotions need to be kept at bay. After that, there is a need to stop everything for a while to be able to think. Afterward, you can reflect on your options and choose the best option.

This type of self-control strategy involves some necessary skills called executive functions. Most children with ADHD do have problems carrying out these skills.

Having some challenges with controlling oneself can also make being empathetic a difficult task. This is because empathy exceeds caring about others. It's also about taking their needs into consideration.

The group of children who can control themself often stop to have a moment to think about how their anger affects others. They might use the insight they gain to keep their anger in check and control the outburst.

But children with ADHD do not find it easy to control themselves without training, but as soon as they calm down and take some time to think, they feel terrible about their actions and how they have made others feel. These negative emotions may build up and later affect their self-esteem and condition.

ADHD and other coexisting conditions

ADHD and other conditions do cooccur together. One of such is anger and anxiety that were earlier mentioned. When a child is worried and anxious about an event and is already at the tipping point, it doesn't take much stimulation for them to tip over into anger.

Children with ADHD do find it difficult to deal with emotions generally. They tend to be fixated on their feelings. If any they are sensitized by any situation, they become tensed and carry the emotion around.

ADHD is also linked with other mental health issues besides anxiety which also is the drive for extreme reactions. These include oppositional defiant disorder (ODD) and depression. You must consult your child's doctor about potential mental health issues as well.

ADHD children may also have some underlying learning issues that are yet to be diagnosed. This may be one of the reasons why schooling is difficult and frustrating for them. This later results in angry outbursts that could have been otherwise prevented and well managed.

Some concerns about ADHD medication

Medications used for ADHD can be very effective in helping some children with their impulsivity. It can also be used for managing irritability and anger. However, these medications do not seem to be effective for all children concerned. Sometimes it even causes more problems and makes them more emotional and irritable.

If this is the case with your child, you must inform your child's doctor. Most times, ADHD medication needs some modifications according to age, body size, and weight for it to be effective.

What you can do to help

Sometimes the most difficult thing about managing your child's anger is staying calm. Equipping your child with the necessary tools to recognize and manage anger can give both of you the necessary control you desire over situations. Below are some of the things you can try out before, during, and after an anger outburst.

You need to note the triggers: Is there a day that your child's control over anger is reduced? Or a situation he can't just tolerate. Knowing what sensitizes your child can help you anticipate the problems and communicate about them before they happen. Triggers could be just that he is hungry and tired. Identifying all these is the first step.

Try to explain what you have observed: Children with ADHD often lose awareness of situations in the heat of the moment. You can help your child to recognize his emotions by calmly saying words like " You seem angry" or "Do you know how loud your voice is?"

Display empathy to build empathy: You must acknowledge that you need to show you understand your child if you want him to understand you. You can try to bring him close to you by coming down to his level of understanding and creating an enabling environment for understanding to take place.

Engage not your child's anger: When your child is furious and acting up, try not to show that you are concerned. Just make sure that everybody is safe and that everything is still under control. You must take charge of the moment and give no place to the anger. You can say, "As you can see, this situation is spiraling out of control, we should calm things down, you can go to your room, and I will go to mine, after some minutes, we will talk again."

Take your time before you talk about the anger episode:

Some children with ADHD find it difficult to be reflective when the situation is happening. You should help your child by giving him some time to think about what happened before talking about it.

When you help a child with ADHD to understand and manage his anger, you don't just help yourself or the home; you also help him to boost his self-esteem and build better relationships.

If your child seems infuriated and frustrated with a high level of anxiety, you can make use of an anxiety log or frustration log to note down the progress of behavior and track the behavioral patterns.

Chapter 7:
ADHD and Dyslexia

Dyslexia is a type of learning disability that impacts a person's language ability and makes reading, spelling, decoding, word recognition, and learning hard nuts to crack. Due to this reading, vocabulary, comprehension, and general knowledge are reduced compared to other children of similar age without dyslexia.

It should be noted, however, that dyslexia does not affect the level of intelligence. Most individuals with dyslexia have a normal or higher than normal intelligence. It has been found that children with ADHD are also likely to develop dyslexia, especially those on the attention deficit side of the spectrum.

How to differentiate between ADHD and dyslexia

It can be very hard to delineate between the challenges related to ADHD and dyslexia since both are neurobehavioral disorders. Knowing that ADHD affects attention and dyslexia affects reading processes, the presenting behaviors may appear the same. Below are three examples.

A peep at distraction

Both ADHD children and those with dyslexia can seem to be distracted, but their distractions are different. An ADHD child might look distracted because it is hard for them to be focused, while a child who is dyslexic will look distracted because reading demands a huge amount of effort, which drains their energy.

Fluency when reading

Someone who reads fluently is a person who reads with accuracy, needed speed and when reading very loud, does so with the needed expressions given to the words spoken. To facilitate understanding of what is being read, the child must be able to read with fluency.

An ADHD child might be poor when it comes to fluency when reading because of their high energy, so they tend to lose the reading pace or skip words because the brain works so fast that the mouth can't catch up. But when it comes to someone who is dyslexic, he is very slow at reading. He takes each word slowly or reads them with the wrong pronunciation.

The way writing is done

Putting words down through writing, also called penmanship, might also become a problem for people with both conditions. The individual with ADHD may have issues with organizing his writeups and proofreading them, while a dyslexic child will, on the other hand, battle with word spellings, organization of his ideas, and writing properly.

A way one can distinguish between these two conditions is to know that problems with dyslexic children are majorly reading and writing activities while ADHD children's conditions are more behavioral, and their symptoms are spread across diverse settings, including academics.

Co-occurring conditions

Before now, Dyslexia and ADHD have been seen as unrelated and without ties. But now, with recent researches and findings, it is clear that impairments in executive functioning, which are mostly seen among those with ADHD, can also be seen with those with dyslexia.

The diagnosis

These two conditions are in real-life diagnosed independently of each other and most times by different professionals. ADHD is seen as a disorder of mental functions and is often diagnosed by psychiatrists, psychologists, and family doctors.

While dyslexia is, on the other hand, noticed and identified by teachers, who will then refer to a medical doctor or a psychologist for further evaluations and diagnosis.

In real life, a clinical psychologist or educational psychologist who can also be a school psychologist is the first point of contact for the diagnosis of dyslexia.

The degree of complexity of the two conditions ranges from mild to severe, which implies that no two people share the same symptoms. There is always a variation at one point or another.

Management for these conditions

For people with dyslexia, there are several special dyslexia reading programs. These programs often adopt some elements from the approach of Orton-Gillingham. This approach is a way of teaching designed to help students with reading problems, specifically dyslexia students. Other research-based materials can also help a dyslexic child with difficulties with reading, spelling, and writing.

Schools have specially trained teachers who can help your child grow past his dyslexic difficulties. But, this is not in all the schools. So, if this is your case, you can just get a special tutor to help out in after-school sessions.

There are also schools with accommodations that provide the necessary home support for ADHD and dyslexic children to help them achieve their academic and life potentials.

How can you increase your child's confidence?

Too on the list of challenges faced by children with dyslexia and ADHD is a low level of confidence and low self-esteem. Most of these children do not feel too good about themselves. Their level of confidence and low self-esteem is further lowered as they unsuccessfully struggle with tasks that their colleagues are doing with ease.

Explained below are three things that you can do to help your child:

- **Tell them the names:** It helps children when they know the name of their condition. It serves as a shield as they confront their friends who try to put them down. They can understand the reason for their behaviors as they learn more about their condition. This prevents them from looking for explanations they already know.

- **Encourage the effort without focusing too much on the results:** You should motivate your children and support their attempts. You should praise them for the energy they put in for a task, not wait till the results. You should know that an ADHD and a dyslexic child do put in more effort for a task than other students, even though these do not always reflect in their grades. When they see that you appreciate their effort, they tend to be confident at putting forth more effort, thereby increasing their self-esteem.

- **Encourage outside of school activities:** If your child is interested in other activities outside the school settings, you should encourage them instead of insisting they excel at school activities. Their ability to showcase their confidence and excellence at something, even if it is boxing, soccer, or arts, helps build their confidence. This will also affect other areas of their life.

Just like other learning disabilities, it is yet uncertain if there is a cure. But, they can be effectively managed in a way that your child will be able to live a satisfying and rewarding life.

You can also encourage them to make role models of famous individuals and celebrities who have faced difficulties similar to what they are currently facing. This will help them have hope and assurance in a better life.

Get help early

It is important to know that effective management of ADHD and dyslexia is assured when there are early detection and early seeking of management. Nonetheless, if you were late discovering that your child has these conditions, you should not feel discouraged or downtrodden. You should know that it is never too late to get out now and seek the needed intervention.

Chapter 8:
ADHD and boredom

You need to know first of all that boredom is not part of the symptoms of ADHD. It is just one of the common after-effects of ADHD, and its behavioral manifestation is often confusing.

This example will shed more light on this; James is a diagnosed ADHD patient who is a schooler. In the class, he is one of the most troublesome. His teachers think that he chooses to disturb the class and often resort to sending him to the principal for disciplinary action after they have tried their best at correction but to no avail. On getting to the principal, the reason James gives for his behavior is that the class was just too boring for him, and he needed to do something to make it lively.

Most children can endure such feeling till the end of the class or until a new subject is introduced by the teacher. This is not the same with children with ADHD. They cannot stand it. They can't control themselves when everywhere becomes too bored for them. It is either they lose their cool or start looking for attention somewhere else.

You also need to remember that children with ADHD are not free of giving different complaints even they were given the autonomy to behave the way they want. This is when you hear some of them say, "the weekend is always boring. I don't even like it when school goes on break."

This does not in any way imply that your child is just too lazy or was just trying to be honest. It is just that he is quite ignorant of how he can prevent himself from being bored without getting into trouble.

ADHD brain and boredom

ADHD children are naturally driven towards getting excitement and liveliness. They are interested in getting fun. It is not that it is their normal personality. Research findings have indicated that their structural and biochemical makeup of the brain is responsible for this

Take a good look at a junior school teacher aiming to get the class's interest in one of the revised writings of Shakespeare. Normally, all the children in the class will find it a bit dull, but because they know they need to know it to be able to pass, they try their best to give it their attention and focus

Children with ADHD are not equipped with that level of control. The reason may be that the regions of the brain that assist them with focusing attention on an object and not be too bored and not well sensitized. They are not functioning as much as those of their friends and neighbors.

The brain also is not actively activating neurotransmitters that make engagement in such activities satisfying, so they are not motivated to give them their focus. This resumes boredom for children with ADHD.

There is one other necessary factor that must be considered to be able to fully understand the ADHD brain and boredom. Children with ADHD are popularly known to have it hard when it comes to making use of their executive skills or the brain's way of managing things.

ADHD children are always glowing with grand ideas about different kinds of interesting things they would love to do. But, you will see them low when it comes to planning, organizing, and executing these grand ideas. They are quite poor in executing their ideas.

Is there anything you can do when your child is filled with complaints about boredom?

You need to understand that boredom is not bad all the time. Therefore all children, including those with ADHD, must learn how to deal with them to a certain extent.

ADHD children might take their time to think about what they can do to come out of their boredom, so what you need to do as a parent is to give your child the time he needs to think about those ideas and execute to the best of his ability before you interfere with your own set of ideas. You should allow your son to grow up and have fun without you being there all the time.

But there are still some things that you can do to help your child manage his boredom or at least minimize it as a parent.

You can create an enabling structure by planning different activities for an after-school session or during the weekend

You should also motivate your child to plan on his own. You should support him in designing the plans and organizing them. You should also plan the timing of your activities together with each of you, giving your consent to the decision made.

However, you should not just close the door on all of your activities just because you want to help your child out. You can invite him to join you in any of your activities; for example, you can call him to plant the garden grass with you or serve dinner together.

You can also be flexible with your guidelines and restrictions. You must not be rigid on them, especially when your child is complaining that he is bored.

You can also find out more about different exciting activities that you can do when indoors so that your child will not be sick of staying inside the house.

Chapter 9:
ADHD and Mood swings

You should know by now that most children with ADHD often have difficulties with managing their emotions. This means they are prone to have unstable emotions, which are also called mood swings. This kind of emotional rollercoasters makes the family members, friends, and neighbors speechless as to the reason behind the sudden changes.

Most children are moody most times and, for the greater portion of these times, cannot control their temper. This is commonly found among teenagers and adolescents. Others can control their mood to some extent. When these children spill some things by mistake or are instructed to put an end to the video game they are so much engrossed in and get back to their schoolwork, they become suddenly enraged.

Children with ADHD tend to be susceptible to feelings of anger, anxiety, disappointment, or frustration like other kids. It may also be the same for other positive reactions.

Also, it is observed that they usually have difficulty controlling themselves with how they react. Their lack of control does not allow them to be able to keep things in perspective. Contrary to this, they may feel minor frustrations are a major problem.

How you can assist with the mood swings

When your child's emotions are taking him on a merry ride, the other members of the family may find it difficult to cope and understand. However, there are still things you can do to help your child manage his emotions.

You must not act in anger or overreact: After your child might have reacted annoyingly because he is bored, you mustn't be quick to react or be so incensed by his behavior. You should understand that flaring up may make your child find it more difficult to get the needed control. And again, your child might lose interest in what you have to say. Hence, you should allow him to vent his anger as long as the expression is not severe.

Think about what you have observed: When your child's irritating mood persists, it will be good if you draw their attention to the here and now so he can catch himself in the act. This may help them to know that they have a mood swing and be able to identify what they are feeling. Getting them to notice their feelings in a calm unbiased way will help them to make a constructive decision.

You can just say that it seems that "you are infuriated about something. You were having a good time earlier." This keeps the conversation in check and helps show them what they are feeling.

Your child may not be ready to discuss his feelings, and you need to respect that. You have to give him space to think about it and reveal the story behind the explosion of his own volition.

Communicate your thoughts about his behavior: It might be that you are worried about making your child feel guilty or ashamed, but your child must be aware that his mood swing is also affecting others, including yourself.

Your child might talk about the way he is feeling, and when he does, do try and empathize with him and let him know that you will like to help him with all his troubles, but this does not mean you should be disrespected.

Be conscious of the ADHD medication side-effect: It might just be that your child's mood swings result from the medication he is taking, especially when this keeps happening around at almost the same time each passing day. ADHD stimulants get eliminated from the system late in the afternoon or towards the evening. Sometimes, this may be the reason why your child is moody. If that is the case for your child, you may detect that your child is just feeling too sad or easily irritated for no good reason.

Finally, children with ADHD have a higher tendency to be anxious or depressed, and these can be responsible for mood swings. Please, try and consult your child's physician if the mood swings persist for more than a week or two.

Chapter 10:
Managing ADHD at home

Up until now, you have been made to understand several problems that a child with ADHD faces and the reasons for these problems. These problems can be perceived from two angles, the physical and the psychological. The psychological problems are those responsible for the unusual behaviors but are caused by the physical ones.

In what ways should a parent handle these problems?

It can be said that the child is the one responsible for his behavior if the problem is psychological, but if these behaviors are absent, the child should be praised, and if the other way round, he should be punished. Also, when the problem is a physical one, the child is not to be held responsible for his behavior, and because of this, it is not right to reward him if they were good or punish him if they were bad.

Another thing is that the child's behavior might be affected by his temperament, but it is not the only determinant for their behavior. Temperament may even affect how easy the child learns to control himself or how easy he can listen to corrections and discipline, but beneficial effects can be achieved by how the parent feels about the child and how he is treated.

Within these past few years, psychologists and psychiatrists alike have discovered that those whose psychological problems result from physical cause can benefit tremendously from some psychological interventions.

These interventions rely on three principles, namely;

- That the patient should be made responsible for their actions.
- They should be rewarded for behaving well, and
- Should be punished (in a defined way) for behaving in the wrong way

A child with ADHD fares well when he is made to be responsible for his behaviors and held accountable for them. He is not be allowed to say, whether directly or indirectly, in so many words giving unnecessary excuses that "I have ADHD, I can't think well, so I cannot be held responsible for my behavior."

He should be made to know that he is responsible and will be held accountable for his actions. This may be communicated by saying, " It is true that you have some problems that are making it so difficult for you to control yourself, but that is very true of everyone else." Everyone out there can do some things easier than other people will do them.

You too, as one of them, can learn to control yourself, count to five and control your temper, not testing your sister all the time, these I expect you to do. You can change these words to your choice as long as it is effective.

The child must not be allowed to either be irresponsible or worthy of blame but should also be dealt with as someone who tends to do well and not be doing bad all the time. He should be treated as someone who tends to be faced with difficulties than normal average children. Patients need to know that there is yet to be a strategy to help eliminate the major ADHD symptoms.

Parents need to remember that the child will be more attention-seeking and forgetful than other children and will behave like he is absentminded and intentionally disregarding the patient's discipline. At the worst, he is not doing any of these to annoy you; he does it because of his condition.

Parents should also set a clear line between those symptoms that will be responsible for both parental training strategies and medicine and those that will only respond to the medicine's effects. This will help them to stop trying to use psychological strategies to modify things that might not respond or might have little response to such interventions.

These symptoms that do not ameliorate psychological interventions include reduced attention span, high level of distraction, moodiness, lack of maturity, etc. These may also cover some behaviors such as bed soiling and wetting, stealing, and other antisocial actions.

Although these problems in the child may not be eliminated by these psychological interventions, they can modify them. For example, a child may continue to show tantrums in his behavior but can be helped to rechannel the energy to other activities when the tantrum is in play.

Summarily, ADHD children's parents need to understand three things. One is that the child will have some difficulties in doing and not carrying out some activities. The second is that he will be helped the most to face and deal with his problems when he is treated like he is responsible for his behaviors, meaning he has the power to continue or leave them whenever he chooses.

The third one is that the degrees to which he can be helped regarding different problems by different parenting strategies differ. It is quite easier to train him on how he controls his anger or how he can be responsible for his actions than to train him to have an increased attention span or reduce his level of distraction. But, both proper medication use and the right discipline will help the most.

Fundamental approach

The major problem an ADHD child has at home is based on discipline. To discuss the fundamental procedures that will help the child function well in a home environment, there is a need to show how the parent can establish the beneficial rule for the child's progress. Thereafter the description of the necessary rewards and punishment that will likely ensure that the child gets better will follow.

Setting the Rules

There are volumes of considerable evidence that supports that some prescribed way of training a child with ADHD is much more effective than others. It has been discovered that if the home environment is firm, defined, consistent, but a little bit predictable, it is best for children with ADHD. Below is a brief explanation of these features.

When it is said the home must be firm, this means that the rules set for the child are that every action has a consequence. When a rule is broken, he is to be punished, and the punishment must always be the same. In the same vein, if he follows prescribed instructions, he must always be praised and acknowledged.

For the home to be consistent, it means that the rules established must remain unchanged from one day to another. As long as he is living in the house with you, if the rule demands that he is to clean and make tidy his room before stepping out to play or do anything, then it must be so without any exception.

The rule should be defined means the rule should be clearly stated, understood, and agreed on by both parties. As an example, time for waking up is 6:00 am, and he should take his bath, clean his room, ensure that his clothes are well hanged in the closet, or that his toys have been returned to their place or that he should make his bed or that he should dust and make clean his room. For this type of rule about cleaning, the rules to be followed must be defined and clear so that both the instructor, the parent, and the child, may have a clear understanding.

When the rule is required to be a little bit predictable, this means that some expected behaviors may have not been mentioned before the rules were established but are required to be fulfilled. The most essential thing is that rules should be enforced after they are made, or else their purpose is defeated. The child is expected to clean his room, make sure his teeth are brushed, ensure other household chores and assignments are completed.

These rules should be enforced in the event of any violation, like taking him to areas where the rules can be obeyed or removing all obstacles to obedience to the rule. This enforcement should be done only when the rules have been established, not beforehand.

Taking a critical look at all these suggestions, some may see it as harsh and sheer wickedness. They also may seem contradictory to several other permissive guidelines that teach that these children should be allowed to behave anyhow they want and that there should be a leveled plane of agreement and discussions between the parent and the child about how things should be done.

These misconceptions need to be addressed; **first of all**, being firm does not directly mean you are harsh. When you display harshness, you are severely and forcefully enforcing your rule on another person. It is just not firmness that will make someone who was arrested for driving too fast be imprisoned for life; that is simply harshness. What firmness will do is to levy the person continually as he repeats such.

Secondly, there is no way you will effectively train a child without a defined structure. Rules and instructions are essential to nurturing them. Also, there is the need for values, norms, and goals to ensure that they can live well. Having a structure does not mean the child is not free; it simply means he is trained to live independently in life.

Every society has rules, regulations, and by-laws which guides the action of those within it. These rules are in place so that there might be orderliness and efficient societal functioning. In adult society, it is wrong to steal, fight indiscriminately, drive when drunk, or embezzle public finances. Adults are not expected to urinate in the open. Abiding by these rules is beneficial to the people themselves.

The first benefit is that it keeps them safe. Also, these rules have direct advantages to those who abide. For someone who has not yet learned how to control his impulses expends a lot of his energy trying to control himself. An alcoholic who is now reformed tries all his best to make sure he does not go back to consuming alcohol. When he is now optimally free, he uses the free energy available to work on other productive activities.

This theory is also in agreement with the rule of self-expression and creativity, which requires one who is smart to focus his energies on greater productivity. A man is seen to be productive by the number of works he can do and his achievements.

A rule that is firm and consistent does not directly relate to the child's self-expression or with how clear the parent and the child will understand each other. The concern has been on rules that will motivate a positive change in behavior, not rules that will influence feelings and thoughts.

These abstracts are quite different from behavior in that they are very difficult to regulate or manage, and parents are advised not to try to do so. Instead, parents should assist their children in expressing and validating their thoughts. However, both the parent and the child should not discriminate during expressions of thoughts and feelings.

To explain realistically, the parents of an ADHD child should not prevent him from expressing his jealous feelings towards one of his siblings, but he should be prevented from harming that sibling of his in any way.
The feeling of getting jealous is quite different from the act of harming.

Finally, the establishment of a firm and consistent rule should not in any way disturb the beneficial conversations that should exist between the parent and the child. This is because, as the child grows older, interactions such as this will form the crux of the family life. At the same time, these discussions are quite helpful to the child.

The child may also make use of these interactions to suggest better ways of carrying out the tasks given to him by the established instructions and in such a way that it will not compromise these instructions. This should be encouraged and highly welcomed. However, the discussions should not give way to hindrances to the formation of corrective rules. They may influence the mechanism of implementation of the set rules and modifications of used terms, but they should not influence how with their defined and consistent enforcement. What should be done and how it should be are influenced by what the parents prefer and what the child suggests.

Theoretically, it is the parent's responsibility to make rules and make their children live according to those rules. Every culture has different vast rules, regulations, and standards to guide the way they behave and each of these cultures has a model that is adapting well to its values. Often, the set of rules and their enforcement demands consistency also on the parts of the parents. Once the child starts growing up to maturity, the parents often get relaxed in setting rules for their children. Now, this is the issue, the young child is only aware of how things are done within his family, but the older child is well informed about how things are run in other families, which may make him rebel against his parent's standards, especially if they seem too stringent.

A mother can fill the food pack of her two-year-old with sweets and biscuits, but doing that for a fifteen-year-old will be met with ridicule on the part of the teenager. When these rules are enacted early in the life of the child, it encourages reception and motivates continuity despite been exposed to different standards outside the family.

The strategies that will be discussed work much more effectively on young children. These methods demand that the child is still dependent on the parent and that the parent also has a certain level of control over the child. This approach may not be effective for those that are independent of their parent.

When dealing with young children, the **first thing** to do is decide vividly and actually what behaviors demand change and copying. The parent must be very clear and straightforward so that the rules might be easy to comprehend and adhere to. Below are some vague and meaningless rules and ways in which they can be clarified:

A. "Your room must be cleaned"- As stated earlier, this instruction can mean so many things. If by the rule the parent is trying to tell the child to do away with every dirt and disorderliness and what the child could only understand from this is to make his bed, the child might feel maltreated if he was criticized after making his bed. According to his standard, his room has been cleaned but not by his parents.

B. "You should observe your table manners." This statement might mean several things according to the standard of the parent. It could mean eating with your fork in place of your fingers or that he say please before reaching out for anything on the dining table, or that he should put a napkin on his laps. This can mean several things in the mind of the child. It is better to be plain to motivate the right compliance and unnecessary negative emotion.

C. "You need to treat your little sister well" This may mean that he should not hurt her in any way or that he should allow her to play with her dolls, or that he should fight back or hit back when she does hit him.

D." You need to be neat all the time" This might also mean that his face must always be clean, or his teeth must always be clean, or that his shirt must not get dirty.

Not only is it that the child is ignorant of what the parent is trying to pass across to him though he can and will argue with his parent in the best of ways about what was the main thing being passed while it is understandable that the parent will also try to make their points and may find it difficult to know if progress has been made.

The **second duty** of parents is to ensure a hierarchy to motivate compliance with the rules. The parent must determine what is right and what is nice for the child. They should also decide what will be important and what will be trivial for the child. They are the ones to give preeminence to a rule above the other. The parent is also the one who sets the punishments for disobedience to the rules.

For example, some parents have been known to be good talkers, and they use their words as punishment on their children. This is highly practiced in some cultures, and some do use restrictions for punishing their children who decide not to complete their assignment. The usefulness of setting the rules with the highest priority is that it assists the parents in focusing on those areas that have more importance before others.

After the most important ones have been controlled, the parents can now move to the next rule in line. One other task for the parents is to determine whether they will abide by their own recommended course of action. This kind of thing is not very easy to do. Sometimes each parent devises their course of action, which most of the time is not very successful in managing an ADHD child, with each having a varying belief about which method will work for the child. For such an environment, the child's problem will continue to persist because of how the parents are managing the situation. This kind of home environment contradicts the unity that is the most essential commodity for helping a child with ADHD to control his actions.

The parents don't have to have a common agreement about the steps to take; they simply need to support each other in their course of action. When the parents are not able to be united in their decisions and are not able to reach a common ground when it comes to acting together to help with their child's behavior, then they can seek out professionals for psychological support. These professionals will help them to thrash out their disagreements and assists them in determining the home rules and how to prioritize the rules according to their importance. This is necessary for the life of the child to progress.

Plan of how rewards and punishments will be

Together with coming up with a set of rules to help the child, parents of ADHD children should predetermine a solid plan of rewarding and punishing their child's behavior.

The decision that will be made and will be considered as a reward and punishment should not only be regarded as such by the parents alone but also by the child. For some individuals, reward and punishment have different meanings. In some associations, the reward is seen as bribery and punishment as brutality. But as far as reward and punishment are concerned in this current context, it means something the child loves so much for the reward such as attention, special privilege, toys, and different others.

Also, as regards the punishment, these are simply things the child doesn't like, such as spanking, denial of privileges, restrictions, neglect, etc.

Generally, for most young children, the most effective and harmless punishment is to use what is called a timeout which is when the child is sent to the room until he is ready to behave in the desired way, such as finishing an assignment, etc. You can just simply say, " You can please go to your room and return for supper when you are done with that assignment," this is an easy way of yelling at your child and ensuring obedience.

There are other two necessary principles of reward and punishment. Number one on the list is that a reward and a punishment should be administered very early. This is because any delay decreases the effectiveness of the process. When your child fulfills his task as he is required to do, he must be appreciated on the spot. If he does not do as required, you must punish him at once. You should not offer distant punishments or rewards. These are a punishment that comes like a threat but might not happen, and these are rewards that take like a week or two to arrive

("Daddy will spank you when he gets home"). Second, the one-time rule should be adopted. The parents should learn the habit of saying do or don't only once before rewarding or punishing. If they do not apply this rule, if they give first, second, third, and tenth warnings before acting, their children will learn to commit ten violations before worrying. In the meantime, the parents will have developed sore throats and built up a good deal of angry steam. In some cases, the child may have been anxiously pushing his parents to take a stand. Surprisingly, most children are relieved when the parent finally acts. A good deal of friction can be avoided by the use of this one-time rule

Secondly, there is a need to adopt the one-time rule— this the act of only saying your command once before rewarding or punishing your child. If this rule is not applied and you resort to giving needless warnings for different times before you act, then your child will learn to disobey you on several occasions before worrying.

Also, during these times, you would have developed a loud voice, gotten good at shouting, built up a lot of resilience against anger. And in some scenarios, your child may be pushing you as a parent because he is anxious about fulfilling your task, so as a parent, you need to take a stand. Astonishingly, some children are always relieved when their parents finally decide to take their stand. A lot of time that may be wasted because of parents' inability to take a stand can simply be avoided by making use of the one-time rule.

Chapter 11:
Parenting Strategies for Patients with ADHD

Since ADHD, or ADD as some people call it, is common with children, it's very imperative that every concerned parent acknowledge the effective parenting strategies for those with other medical challenges.

There is a clear difference between raising a child battling with ADHD and one that is not. Some things may be impossible when raising a child with ADHD depending on how severe it is. In this situation, parents are advised to adopt different approaches. Honestly, parents may sometimes feel frustrated when trying to cope with some of the behaviors which result from their child's ADHD; nonetheless, they can find their way around it to make life better by adopting some specific strategies.

First and foremost, parents must know and accept that the brain of a child with ADHD is different from the brain of one who doesn't have it in regard to functionality. A child with ADHD is highly susceptible to impulsive behavior, even though such a child can still learn what is passable and want isn't.

To help a child with ADHD, parents must look for ways to modify their behavior and learn to manage the child. There are two specific ways to treating a child with ADHD: use of medication and adopting behavioral techniques. For every adopted method for managing the symptoms of a child's ADHD, behavioral techniques must be in place.

According to Dr. Paul Jenkins, the author of Pathological Positivity, Attention deficit hyperactivity disorder (ADHD) happens to fall under "a very complicated constellation of symptoms." You cannot carry out a blood test to examine and know if a child has it. The diagnosis of ADHD in children is based on two things: symptoms and observation. It may sometimes be very confusing as the symptoms or what we observe in a child with ADHD may also be seen in most children, that is, what they do "at least occasionally to some level." Dr. Paul says, "So when we make a diagnosis of ADHD, it's because many of these symptoms are appearing at a level that is higher than we would expect from most kids. Having said that, I think we over-diagnose it in our society, and there are cases that we miss. But either way, it's a challenging constellation of behaviors."

According to Dr. Paul, there are basic principles that parents must understand which can make a great difference in the child's life with ADHD. These principles are tied to two important concepts that interact and affect each other. These are control and maturity.

- **Control**: Dr. Paul says, "Control means control over your own life. It goes from 0 to 100% control, so you can have all of it or none of it or somewhere in between."
- **Maturity**: Dr. Paul says, "maturity has to do with how grown-up you are. But it's not just by age; it's about the stage."

There are three stages of maturity — stage 1, stage 2, and stage 3. The relationship between maturity and control in this area is that the level of your maturity will determine how much control you have— "...the least mature you are, the less control you have. The more mature you are, the more control you have." Children are still incapable of taking full control of their life because of the level of their maturity, and this explains why parents must try to share the control.

Going back to the stages of maturity, the first stage (**stage 1**) refers to the least mature. Children can easily be identified to fail the first stage when they exhibit some actions such as defiance, opposition, fighting, tantrums, demanding, and screaming. Stage 1 is an immature level. These behaviors may be considered appropriate for children (toddlers to two years). However, if exhibited by a 16 or 17-year-old, something is definitely wrong somewhere— it's outrightly immature.

The next stage is **stage 2**. This stage is described by Dr. Paul as a stage "where we stop fighting and start cooperating." Cooperation can be placed right on the dividing line existing between the first and the second stages. Dr. Paul expresses, "If your child is cooperating, they are at least on stage 2. Stage 2 is much more pleasant for parent and child because we are working together." At stage 2, there is negotiation. Here, people try as much as possible to stay out of trouble (keeping the peace) by going along with "reasonable requests."

The final stage is **stage 3**. This is a stage of responsibility. The major thing about this stage which should not be forgotten is empathy. Dr. Paul explains empathy as the capacity to "understand and care how someone else feels." If your child falls in this stage, you will see how they understand and show interest in other people's feelings and how your behavior impacts such individuals. According to Dr. Paul, the drivers of behavior on stage 3 include empathy, morals, service, ethics, and values. You will know when your child gets to the third stage. Your child will have more control. Usually, parents tend to withdraw the moment their children reach stage 3. This is because this stage centers on "self-control" and "self-discipline."

The concepts explained above have a lot to do with ADHD and other condition or diagnosis, or syndrome that a child may be dealing with. For children with ADHD, the maturity scale will show how they cannot get much control over themselves. In this situation, parents need to come into the picture and take more control. Besides, if it's about other syndromes where a child suffers from a developmental or pervasive delay that can lower such a child's maturity level, it's very important that someone get in control. Parents are advised to clarify the maturity exchange and control to ensure they are taking the right control level as the parents when dealing with their child with ADHD.

Note, as parents, your job is not to control their lives. Your job is to encourage them toward self-control and maturity via teaching, training, and proper education on how they can run their life in a better way. Dr. Paul says, " Here's what I really like as a practical approach and a big shout out to Foster Cline and Jim Fay authors of, 'Parenting with Love and Logic.' You might be familiar with the Love and Logic people and curriculum and the wonderful materials that they have made available. They are great resources for parents, and I highly endorse what they are doing."

Dr. Paul shared four great steps for parents while dealing with their child that has ADHD, and it's referenced from Foster Cline and Jim Fay. They are as follows:

- **Give the child a task**: This is the first step. Here, parents are to give their child a specific task that such a child can handle.

The confusing part here is that it may be difficult to know certainly that your child can handle it because of their incapacity in the past. However, Dr. Paul claims that if parents become frustrated because their children are not doing something, it means there is a possibility that they can do it. This is because if you know they are not capable, you won't be frustrated. Therefore, this should prompt you to give them a task that they are capable of handling.

- **Hope that they'll blow it:** This is a very great step suggested by Cline and Fay. This step has a lot to do with the brain of a child with ADHD, even though it goes against the normal thought of a parent. From Dr. Paul's explanation, there's much clarity on how this step ties into an ADHD brain— the prefrontal part of the human brain is in charge of regulating behavior, doing logic, thinking rationally, and solving problems. This same part may become lazy in a child suffering from ADHD. So, it may be necessary to wake it up. To do this, you may use the problem-ownership strategy. This implies that the person that feels the weight of a problem owns it. This may not sound very good to some parents because they believe the problem ought to be theirs. Nonetheless, you may want to think about shifting the problem from your side over to the shoulders of the child, but in an appropriate way that such a child can handle. This approach may be effective because if children with ADHD own their problem, it is more likely that they will engage the pre-frontal part of their brain to find solutions to their problems.

- **Allow the consequences to do the teaching**: This step also explains the vital role of empathy. As previously explained, there are two basic components when it comes to empathy: "understand and care how someone else feels." Dr. Paul shows how it's not advisable to clobber them with consequences. The choice of blowing it in the second step leads to the consequences. This is absolutely fine because our intention is to let them learn a specific thing. By the time we get to the third step, consequences are made to fall, and then we introduce empathy. It's also very important that you avoid saying, "I told you so." Don't be sarcastic; the idea will fail. Try to attack the issue with ingenuity, connection, and empathy because they will still face the consequence.

- **Give the child the same task again**: This step is meant to send a powerful message which can help address the challenge that the child with ADHD might be facing. According to Dr. Paul, the message that parents want to pass to their children is that they are smart enough because they have brainpower. They are equipped with the ability to solve problems and learn from the mistakes they may make. Let them know that you know that they have learned from the experience they have and that you will let them try again. This should serve as an incentive for them to think.

It's important to know that ADHD can influence how people think and reduces their level as far as the maturity scale is concerned. This step is useful for making the life of a kid with ADHD better.

Parents that have a child battling with ADHD should try to ensure that they employ a good approach. The life of your child can incredibly be transformed if you make some changes to your parenting strategies— it can equip the child with the appropriate tools needed to manage effectively the way they behave.

Characteristically, a child with ADHD is impulsive, spontaneous, and free-spirited. There are lots of challenges parents will go through while trying to bring up a child with ADHD. However, there are ways they can support their child in developing positive behavior. Every concerned parent should try to come up with specific ways of interacting with their child. This may be in relation to gestures, speech, the physical environment, and emotional language.

To help a child with ADHD, the parents need to be consistent in using a structured and supportive approach. This will greatly help minimize the child's challenging behaviors and make such a child live a flourishing life.

Parents can help minimize their child's disruptive behaviors and other challenges that such child may be facing that have to do with ADHD by observing the following parenting tips for ADHD.

- **Make challenging activities interesting**: It is observed that children with ADHD usually get distracted if they are not given a complex task to handle. "Distractibility" is a common phenomenon that parents should try to deal with using strategies such as encouraging, giving praise, and occupying them with tasks that are challenging.

  Hyperfocus is the opposite of distractibility. Hyperfocus simply refers to the situation in which children are so focused that they become unaware of what's happening around them. Apparently, it may be very challenging for a child to be hyperfocused, but it's how a child can deal with important tasks.

There are several jobs and hobbies that demand a high level of focus. As a parent, if you observe that your child finds challenging activities interesting and can focus while getting them done, what you need to do is to encourage such a child to continue.

It's also very important that parents reinforce the good behavior of a child with ADHD with praise. This is a way of passing a message across to such a child about the acceptable behaviors (those receiving praise) and the unacceptable ones.

Moreover, another way by which parents may minimize sudden distractions is by providing structure with a daily schedule. Children with ADHD can be calm if they are with the knowledge of what to expect. It's a great way to make a child responsible.

- **Encourage Exercise**: Exercising is an excellent way to burn off excess energy. When excess energy finds its way out of the body, it reduces the risk of anxiety and depression, promotes focus and concentration, improves sleep patterns, and stimulates the brain.

One of the best ways parents can assist children with ADHD is to encourage physical activity. You can get them active toys (such as skipping ropes and balls), enroll them in a team sport, or teach them how to ride a bike.

Parents can also passively assist them by merely being good role models in the area of physically active habits. If parents are great in this area, children can be influenced. Playing outdoors together or going on family hiking can help children with ADHD burn excess energy and develop healthy habits.

- **Getting good quality sleep**: Practicing good sleep hygiene can go a long way in helping a child with ADHD. According to research, it's claimed that low quality sleep can contribute negatively to ADHD symptoms. However, to regulate energy levels, good quality sleep can be required. Good sleep can also reduce the level of stress and improve the mood of a child with ADHD. Therefore, parents should ensure that they add regular bedtime hours to the plan they have for their children for the day.

- **Break tasks into achievable goals**: Children with ADHD can see some tasks to be too complex and off-putting. To assist them, parents can try to break their tasks into goals that they can achieve where possible. For instance, if you ask a child with ADHD to clean the room, you can divide this task into smaller segments, such as folding the clothes, putting any toys on the floor into storage, and making the bed. This system can be a very helpful one.

- **Get them to pause and express their thoughts aloud**: Children with ADHD are characterized by a lack of impulse control. This implies that they may do or say something without first thinking about it. Parents can come in here to get them to pause and express aloud what they think about. This strategy comes with several benefits. It can offer the child enough time to consider their thought before taking any action (if it's good to act or not to act on them). It can also help the parents to learn the thought patterns of their child.

- **Try to minimize distractions**: keeping distractions to a minimum can be helpful. If you discover that your child is easily distracted, you can try to ensure that the surroundings are uncluttered. Ensure you know what your child prefers between televisions or radios—you may want to turn any of these off or down to keep them focused. They may focus if you get them to handle challenging tasks while you keep them away from games or TV. Besides, you will want to put away their toys when they are in their bedrooms doing something that needs to be done.

- **Adopt the explanatory method, not the imperative method**: You can help a child with ADHD by explaining why some tasks are done or need to be done in vivid and positive language. Checking that the child's age is appropriate, parents or caregivers can present to such a child the reason for what they're asking. Ensure that the reason is simple and be ready to explain when asked to expatiate.

  Giving a good explanation of why a task is done can alleviate confusion and worry in a child with ADHD. It's very important that when you decide to explain things, your language use must be completely clear and positive.

  Moreover, it's respectful when you explain why you ask a child to carry out a specific task; mind you, self-respect is vital if the child has the feeling of being different from others.

- **Introduce wait time**: Every parenting strategy is unique in its own way. Wait time and thinking out loud are similar. Introducing wait time can help a child manage their actions. If children with ADHD wait for some seconds before acting or speaking as a thought runs through their minds, they may have enough time to consider their actions ("are they appropriate or not"). This is a strategy that requires lots of practice, but the benefits make it worthwhile. Introducing wait time can offer children with ADHD a real advantage in how they live their lives socially.

- **Avoid getting overwhelmed**: Everyone has their elastic limit. Parents tend to get overly stressed sometimes, which affects their well-being and their capability to support their kids effectively.

  Parents should not find it difficult to ask for support if they discover that their obligations and workload are becoming too overwhelming. They can seek help from family, friends, or local ADHD support groups capable of rendering needed support. Actually, you can reduce your stress by taking one thing out of your weekly schedule.

- **Do not use negative language**: Parents should endeavor to always offer a child with ADHD positive feedback. This is a great way to help the child build confidence.

  Children with ADHD sometimes may feel that they are not loved or are not good enough because of the feelings that they always do things wrong. These feelings shouldn't be reinforced with negative language— such negative language can hurt the child and worsen the child's disruptive behaviors.

  It's certain that you won't be positive all the time, especially when you intend to express your worries or concerns. But you can find an outlet to push this out— it might be a therapist, partner, or friend.

  There are also support groups where parents of children with ADHD come together to discuss the challenges they are going through with other parents experiencing similar situations.

- **Give room for appropriate and consistent consequences**: You can't let attention deficit hyperactivity disorder be in control. You need to take proper action when necessary. You may intend to offer allowances to a child with ADHD, but ADHD will not excuse poor behavior. There ought to be boundaries between children and parents, and it's important that children learn that there are consequences from time to time for their actions anytime they misbehave. You should let them know that unruly behavior is not tolerated. Nonetheless, ensure that these consequences are consistent and appropriate. A child with ADHD may feel encouraged to continue uncontrolled or wild behavior if parents fail to follow through on the consequences.

- **Learn to let smaller things go**: Parents can face different challenges posed by a child with ADHD. Such a child may exhibit impulsive and hyperactive behavior. So, if parents of such a child decide to address every problem presented by the child's behavior, it will definitely be a special issue on its own as each day would become stressful and obnoxious for everyone. It's, therefore, important to learn how to forgo some smaller things, which can help alleviate stress and help focus on controlling the more important behaviors.

- **Engage in effective communication with other adults**: Parents of a child with ADHD may be tempted to begin to see other adults as the enemy, but you shouldn't. Naturally, you may feel protective, but you need to know that it will seem other caregivers do not care enough or understand their behavior when children have ADHD.

It's, therefore, good to communicate with people that your child is in contact with about ADHD— make them understand the child's preferences and describe the effective interventions for their challenging behavior.

- **Never stop trying**: Sometimes, it may appear that improvements on the child's condition are stalled, but you shouldn't give up. Keep trying— there are lots of potential in children with ADHD.

  You will be needing a lot of patience and wait for positive changes. It may take time, but certainly, it will turn out well.

- **Seek professional support**: There are conditions you may find difficult to handle on your own. These kinds of conditions require the assistance of a specialist. There are numerous ADHD therapists who can help parents deal with stress attached to a child's behaviors. Besides, you can find local and national support groups that can be of help. You may also make yourself available for input from other parents experiencing a similar situation— this can ultimately be invaluable.

- **Give yourself breaks**: You do not want to wear yourself out while dealing with your child's behaviors all day long. It's exhausting when you spend the whole day attending to a child. You can take breaks by giving out the job to a babysitter or letting your partner take the responsibilities. It may be difficult to cope with stress if you expend most of the energy you have as a parent.

- **Try to calm yourself down**: One of the best ways to help your brain with problem-solving and better communication is when you remain calm. As parents, you can engage the following strategies to stay calm:

- Practicing yoga
- Meditating regularly
- Reducing alcohol and caffeine consumption
- Walking in calming outdoor space
- Sticking to a specific routine to reduce the stress of "what else to be done?"

- **Understand that every child misbehaves**: People may easily conclude ADHD is responsible for the challenging behavior of a child, but you should understand that every child misbehaves. This will help you know the behaviors that should be managed and those that should be regarded as normal parts of maturity.

- **Treat yourself with kindness**: Parents of a child with ADHD should see themselves as people who are trying their best. They should learn how to appreciate the challenges they have successfully overcome and take pride in their achievements.

Don't be tempted into thinking that other parents are doing great and better than you. Actually, when you talk with other parents, you will see that you're really trying. Be kind to yourself and appreciate how far you've gone and how well you have done.

Chapter 12:
How can a parent help their child or adolescent with ADHD

ADHD has been seen as a hereditary disorder for a long while now. It has been a major discourse for many who are interested. The management of the condition has also been a major subject of discussion for some time now.

As a parent interested in taking care of your child with ADHD, managing your child's symptoms effectively is important because it goes a long way in influencing how severe the disorder will be and the possible development of more problems over time. This makes early intervention the best option to choose and a major key for better outcomes for your child.

How soon you can attend to your child's issues determines the likelihood of you being able to forestall disappointments and failures at school and during social activities. There are also some other related issues such as low productivity, underperformance, and low self-esteem, contributing to the development of delinquent behaviors such as indiscriminate drug use and alcohol addiction.

Even though life may be a little bit challenging for you and your child, being a parent, you can be instrumental in positive changes in his life and in creating a supportive home environment and a helping school life for your child. This will increase your child's potential for a happy life.

The life of your child may be riddled with challenges and difficulties and may be very frustrating, but as a parent, you can support him by making the home comfortable and therapeutic for him and facilitating a better school environment that will further improve your child options for success.

Below are some ways that you can find helpful

- **Try not to waste the little energy you have on blaming yourself**

ADHD is a common disorder that affects specific regions of the brain and can be passed down from one generation to another, according to most cases. It is yet to be discovered that one of its causes is due to a poor system of parenting or a home environment filled with chaos, although the environment of the house can make the symptoms of ADHD better or worse.

- **Try to do more research on what ADHD is to learn all that you can**

Even though there is a lot of information out there about the likely causes of ADHD, the method of diagnosing it, and the available treatment modalities, not all these are accurate or based on scientific evidence. It is going to be your responsibility to be a good learner and try to differentiate between the information that is genuine and those that are not.

Ways to differentiate the useful ones from those that are not.

Generally, you have to be very careful of advertisements that are out there with the claim of having a cure for ADHD. As of now, there is yet to be a known cure for ADHD, but as a parent, there are several steps that you can take to decrease its effect.

Also, you need to scrutinize the source of information. When you are using the internet, you must stick with well-known websites like those of the government, such as the site of the United States Center for Disease Control and Prevention (CDC), a nonprofit organization, or university sources (sites whose address ends in .edu)

- **Ensure you get a comprehensive assessment for your child**

You need to get a comprehensive assessment for your child, which involves a medical, educational, and psychological evaluation (which involves getting some suggestions from the teacher of your child) and verifying that there are no other underlying conditions or co-occurring conditions with ADHD.

It might be difficult to be a parent to a child with ADHD. This is because the child will often behave in ways that are very different from those of other children. The child may also have trouble listening to your instructions because of the underlying inattention and high impulsivity.

All these may make things a little bit difficult for you as a parent. This may also make you change some things in your house so that you can help your child. Below are some of the things you can do to help

- **Plan and structure activities within the house**

You need to organize all activities in your house. You will have to come up with specific times that you want your child to be waking up, doing household chores, recreation activities such as playing games and watching TV, and also time to go to bed. This timetable should be written on a piece of paper or a whiteboard and hanged where you can gain easy and continual access to it.

If your child is still yet to learn to read, you can communicate your instructions in the form of drawings or symbols to outline each day's activities. You should notify your child early and explain if there will be any changes in the normal routine. Do make sure that your child understands all that you are communicating.

- **You need to establish house rule**

You should establish a rule of behavior within the house. You need to make these rules for in-house behaviors simple to understand, clear, straightforward, and brief. The rules should be well explained in a clear format.

It is also crucial that you communicate the penalty for breaking the rules and the reward for adhering to them. All of these must be well spelled out and clear to see. When you write the rules down, also write down the penalties to be doled out if they were not followed and the reward to be given if they are adhered to. The penalty should be immediate, consistent, and fair.

- **Stay positive**

You need to let your child know what you expect from him and the things you want him to stop doing. You should reward him constantly for doing what you expect from him and being of good behavior. This may even include small things such as getting him dressed or picking him up early from school with a present. An ADHD child has his day filled with criticism about the things that he is not doing well, so he needs to be appreciated for doing the right things, and this must be continuous and timely.

- **You should ensure that your directives and instructions are well understood by your child**

First, you should try to gain your child's attention, this may be a little difficult because of his condition, but you should encourage him to be attentive to you. Make him look directly into your eyes, then tell him in a straight, plain, and calm manner the specific things you want him to do and how you want him to behave. You can ask him to repeat the directives that were communicated to him back to you. It works well when these instructions are short, clear, and simple. If the task is hard, you should give only one instruction or at most two at a time, then appreciate and reward him for every step he completes.

- **Be consistent**

You should only promise what you will be able to give. You should only communicate the things you are ready to do. Also, avoid repeating instructions and directives; it will slow down compliance from your child. When your child goes against your instructions or disobeys your directives, you should only warn him in a gentle and calm voice once. If the warning is ineffective, you should dole out the penalties that were already outlined. You should beat down to the barest minimum the use of physical punishment as this often complicates the issue.

- **Make sure your child is under supervision at all times**

Due to their high level of hyperactivity and impaired control of impulse, children with ADHD need an adult to be around to supervise and monitor them than other children within the same age group. So, you must put your child under supervision by adults all day long.

- **Observe your child when he is around his friends**

You need to keep an eye on your child when he is with his friends. Children with ADHD find it difficult to learn adequate social skills and obey social rules. You can help your child by choosing playmates for him. It is preferable to select friends with similar verbal and social abilities. You can invite them into the house one or two at most at a time first. Then observe them as they play together. You can use this medium to evaluate his progress and check out the other things that need to be worked on. You should reward good friendship behaviors and playing skills. At the top of it is you must not allow any form of foul play such as yelling, beating, or pushing in your house or its surroundings.

What you can do to help your child with his academics

- **Assume the role of a care coordinator**

You need to start keeping a record of your child's information. This record is compilations of all report cards, notes given by the teacher, reports of disciplinary action, evaluations, and minutes of all meetings attended because of the child. You may also get all your records on ADHD, the documentation of your child's previous training and treatments, and also the contact details of all professionals who have managed your child in the past.

You can also create a team that will include people who understand ADHD, and you should be the captain of the team. You can schedule a meeting in your child's school, and this meeting will be attended by all those under whose care your child is at school. These meetings are to serve as a medium for discussion about how your child can be helped at school. Several other individuals who are part of your team should be requested to give inputs during the meetings based on their understanding of your child's condition.

These well-informed members of the team can include the psychologist working in the school as well as the professional psychiatrist handling your child's condition. You can also make special consultations with some other ADHD specialists in other to gather more necessary details about your child, which you will also make use of during the meetings.

When detailed information is gotten about your child concerning the areas where he is strong and those areas where he is still weak, and how all these are influenced by the presence of ADHD will be valuable to you and also other team members to be able to come up with an effective management plan that has every area put into consideration.

- **You should get informed about the academic rights of your child being ADHD diagnosed**

The more you know about what your child is entitled to under the available laws of education, laws guiding the education of those that are disabled, and his right to rehabilitation, it will go a long way to determine the extent of help you can give to him. The success rate of the management plans also hangs on the balance of the knowledge of this information. There are in every state center which renders technical support for parents. These centers can assist you in your quest to know more about the right of your child.

- **You need to be the number one advocate for your child**

It is your responsibility to be there for your child and represent him wherever you go. You should advocate for his support in all activities of the school, be it educational, social, or physical performance. You should not just assume the ceremonial role of being the team captain but be very active to exercise your powers in deciding the kinds of help your child gets according to available and lawful school assistance.

- **Communicate actively**

You need to be ready to collaborate with other members of your team and show them your readiness to learn and get needed help. The goal of the team is to support your child in every way possible, so you must be at the forefront of making that happen. The school teachers within the team need to know if any changes are going on at home which can affect your child's behavior. You should also create an avenue where your child's school teacher will be able to reach you without any hindrance by advising them to contact you as soon as any issue arises. The existence of an unrestricted means of communicating between you and team members in your child's school will of great help for you and your child.

- **You can be part of a local action group**

As a parent of a child with ADHD, you can also be a member of a local support group where you can meet to discuss available supportive actions. Through the chapter locator, you can locate a nearby chapter to your house.

- **Get professional assistance**

You should also consult professionals in the field of mental health who know more, especially when you are getting discouraged, downtrodden and distressed. You need to be in a good psychological state before you can help your child.

- **Need to cooperate and agree with others**

Everyone who is in charge of taking care of your child in one way or another needs to cooperate and be united in the ways your child is going to be cared for. There might also be a need to work with an ADHD specialist to guide you and advise on the best way you can work together.

- **Gain an understanding of effective behavior management skills.**

It has been established that one of the key components of managing a child with ADHD is to make use of behavior modification strategies. Undergoing training as a parent of a child with ADHD will fortify you with the latest strategies useful in constructively improving your child's relationship. There are available program platforms where the parent of ADHD children can meet and share working techniques as well as learn basic education about the different aspects of ADHD. You can also access different training programs in your community

- **Go for a checkup to see if you have ADHD**

Because ADHD is often inherited, most parents of children with ADHD also find out that they have ADHD too, though they went to diagnose their child's condition. Parents of children with ADHD do need similar types of assessment and management that are also required for their children. The condition may predispose the parents to irrational behaviors as well, which will make the home more distressing and influence the parent's ability to offer due help to their child.

Training as a parent will assist you to know about how to:

Give plain, straightforward, and consistent directions and expectations. ADHD children should understand what their parents expect from them. You need to make this clear to them even though they are often inattentive.

ADHD children get more confused in ambiguous circumstances, especially when they don't understand exactly what to do because of their impulsivity. When you work with a specialist, the right guide on how to go about being an ADHD parent will help you break things down and shed more light on how to go about your parenting strategies.

1. Create a working disciplinary strategy

Creating an active strategy for disciplining your child will promote good behavior. As a parent, you need to learn to cultivate proactive disciplinary methods that motivate and reward positive behavior and deter responses to bad behaviors to motivate change.

You should also communicate with those working with you concerning managing your child's condition at home and at work to have a consistent disciplinary strategy at home and work.

2. Assist your child as he learns from his mistakes

Most times, without any action, consequences are given naturally to bad behaviors. However, ADHD children are unable to understand the connection between their behaviors and the consequences they generate. Parents need to shed light on these connections with their children. This will help the children with ADHD to recognize the impact their behaviors have on others.

3. How do you elevate your child's morale

You need to create a time when you and your child can have a special moment together daily. An ADHD child is continually exposed to criticism and discrimination from every corner, and this impacts his self-perception and leads to a lower estimation of self. Having a special moment together can be in the form of going out to visit places together or performing a task together; these moments should be used to encourage the child and boost his morale. You should be a major source of comfort and support for your child.

4. Appreciate and note your child's success, even if they are small

You should always try to observe and call the attention of your child when he is doing well with so much appreciation, even if it is small. You should inform your child what exactly he did right and motivate him to do more. This will go a long way in elevating his morale and improving his self worth

5. You should let your child know that you love him and will be there for him unconditionally

There will be moments when this will be just a mirage to you. There will be a moment when you will be very sad for yourself and your son. These should be the days you acknowledge the effort of your child, show him love, and appreciate him the more. These are the moment you should be there for your child without wavering. You need to give your child a sure hope of having you as someone to rely on no matter what happens. This will promote positive behavioral change within a supportive environment.

6. Help them to build good friendship skills

ADHD children are often disregarded by friends and schoolmates alike because of their impulsivity, hyperactivity, and lack of attention. When you undergo quality parenting training for the parent of children with ADHD, you will be equipped with the knowledge and skills to help your child learn how to build good social skills.

7. You must acknowledge your child's strength

Many children with ADHD are talented in different areas but are often looked down on by ignorant ones. They do excel in areas such as sports, art, and engineering. You can help your child to develop his ingenuity in any of these areas. This will give so much moral boosting and a feeling of self excellence. You need to create an enabling environment for him to express his skills and talents. You should also encourage him not to allow his condition to undermine his efforts. You should motivate him to focus on these strengths and bring the best out of him. You should encourage him to channel the strengths and boost from these skills to develop other good behaviors, and you should let him know that he can do better. He should be encouraged not to let others discourage him in any way.

Chapter 13:
Things not to Say to an ADHD Child

Parenting a child with ADHD can be likened to trying to crack open a stone with your bare hands. It does feel like you are climbing a mountain top every day, and it seems the mountain keeps getting taller. You continue to put in your best, but nothing seems to be going your way.

A parent of an ADHD child once narrated her ordeal. She said, "I remembered letting all the build-up stress from within one day when I broke down into tears with my young boy. I started crying, and he broke into tears as well. I had to place myself in one corner on the floor, just crying. It was the only thing I could do at that time. After a while, I was able to get calm, and I gave him a piece of my mind, and it was the real truth. At times, you always made me think that I am not a good mom!"

"These words had already escaped my mouth before I could gather myself to think about how terrible they were and how my child might have felt about them. What I said was done so that I might feel relieved as a mother, but rather, it hurt my child and myself. After hurling those words at him and having regained myself at that time, it was too late, he was now in a bad state, and I felt so awful as well. It was then I knew the method I was using will not work. I needed to change things and get better". These are the words of the mother.

As a parent, you will do much good if you can control yourself, take your time to undergo some training, and know more about how ADHD presents itself in children, including their behaviors. It is better for those mouths to be closed than to use them to hurl hurtful words at your child with ADHD. You will only end up complicating the whole situation.

Everyone who understands how it is to have a child with ADHD will want to be very careful with what they say to a child who is having his fair share of the not-so-good side of life by struggling with ADHD condition. But again, it is simple honesty to say that relating or communicating with a child with ADHD takes a lot of mental power and can be quite tiring, making those wrong words you have always been avoiding let themselves out despite trying your possible best to keep them locked in.

Also, it is almost certain that you will meet different types of people as you try to care for your child, some will encourage you, and some will discourage you. Those who discourage are among those who do not know anything about the condition, the difficulties you are facing, your effort over the years to help your child, and the impact that the condition has on your daily life.

Similarly, some do not want to understand at all and are filled with misconceptions about the condition. Some of them believe that ADHD is just a myth that is formulated by some group of people over the years to be able to gain cheap popularity and to impose levies on those parents who are ignorant and easily swayed. Some others think that ADHD is a mild none threatening condition that can be managed with ease by the parents and will later wear off when the child matures into an adult.

This group of people is unaware of the wonderful efforts and responsibilities carried by parents with an ADHD child. One of the responsibilities is the need to control one's emotions despite having to deal with an emotional child. As a parent of an ADHD child, there are times you will be so infuriated, and those provoking words that you are trying to seal in will just be ejected by your anger.

Therefore, you must understand what the things you should let out of your mouth to your child are so that you can be supportive as you want to be and can help yourself and your child. You also need to know the better alternatives to these words to substitute the provocative ones with better ones.

Below are some of the words or statements that you should avoid, whether you are just too angry, short of what to say, or trying to be very careful not to say the wrong words but ended up letting them out.

1. Why behave like this?

There are so many times you will be tempted to ask this question just because, at the moment, you were annoyed with how your child is behaving. It is at this time you will want to furiously question the motives behind such behavior just because, for a moment, your elevated emotions have overclouded your knowledge of his current condition, and you are just frustrated as many other parents will be with the incessant display of truancy.

During this moment which will just happen within less than half of a minute, you need to calm yourself down first, take some steps backward and count some numbers in your head to distract you from the infuriating stimulus, then breath in deeply. At this moment, you need to remind yourself of the condition of your child and remember that he is not behaving that way intentionally. It was not of his willful doing; it is simply because there is something not going well with how his brain is functioning. His mind is not as developmentally matured as you are taking it to be.

2. You can try saying these words instead:

" I could see you are having a bad time currently, and you are finding it difficult to control yourself. Will you prefer that you be left alone for a while?"

If the answer a yes, you will need to excuse him and make sure that he is left alone for a while somewhere to recuperate. You may tell him to go to where he feels he will be comfortable alone; this may be his room or the toy's room. You need to stress it for him to hear and understand that he is not given a time out now or placed on any punishment that it is simply that he deserves time alone to recollect himself and be able to control himself

As a parent, one of the things you need to teach your child is that his emotion is very important, and he should not try to ignore his emotions but rather learn to control them. This is because it will strengthen his ability to deal with emotions and increase his threshold to withstand disturbing emotions. In the long run, because he has learned to control them, he will be emotionally balanced as an adult.

3. You know better!

The truth is he does not; he is very impulsive and prone to making a lot of mistakes because he finds it difficult to keep his body in a place. As a parent, do not make the mistake of believing he understands what he is doing or that he is in control of his emotions and behavior. He does not. You must teach him, instruct him and make him understand by being plain, short, and simple.

Therefore, instead of saying that, you can say this:
"I am not happy with your decision right now, you should know it is not a very good one, and I know you can do better than that." When you say this, and he hears you well, he can understand that you greatly believe in him, have high hopes for him, and that you think as time goes on, he will be able to make better decisions and make himself better.

4. Take it easy

As a parent, you might have finished saying this before realizing the subtle damage it can make. As an adult, if your friend has said this to you in the past, you will understand how such words efficiently domesticate one's emotion. You should know that because of the conditions of an ADHD child, his feelings and emotions are on the high side. ADHD children tend to emote on a deeper and scarier level than other normal children. Again, unlike ADHD children, other normal children have their brains constantly developing to cope with their developing emotions. But, the same cannot be said for those with ADHD. Their brains are not developing at the rate at which their emotions are. They don't have the executive skills to calm themselves down at moments when their emotions are piqued.

5. Instead of you saying that you can do this:

Behave as if you don't mind the emotions. You can, instead of saying that he should take it easy, initiate another activity. You can, for example, try to ask him if he can breathe in deeply as you can do. Normally, he should start an argument about who can take in more breaths. You can then reinforce that by saying, "I am sure you are not as good as I am," this will make him try every attempt to beat you at taking a deep breath. During this time, his attention will have shifted from the infuriating emotion that had made him unstable to you. You can now try to sustain the breath-taking-in competition by taking a deep breath as well. Just make sure that you do not give out any signs that you are disturbed by his behavior in any way. A little shouting can upset the whole activity. Trying to distract his attention without querying the source of the anger goes a long way in calming down both the child and yourself.

6. Stop your stupid cries; I say you should stop

Just like it is not a good thing to say take it easy, it is also not good to tell your child to stop crying. It is like telling a sweeping rain to stop all at once. You know that it will only take a miracle for that to happen. Just like a process that moves with pace or a car moving on a highway, sadness has its own pace, and when it is more than what can be contained, it has to be released. It is a natural response to any inciting or depressing stimulus. Just like other children, those with ADHD also need to express themselves and release internal tension. The only difference is that they may need us to be there for them and understand them whenever they exhibit such responses.

7. Instead of that, you could just say this:

Instead of trying to force them to stop weeping or shout at them to cease their cry, you can just simply say, " I am very sorry you were infuriated; it is very normal for you to react in such a way. You can also try to add to this depending on whatsoever is the reason why they were crying. When you validate the feeling of a child with ADHD, it helps them acknowledge that crying is a normal phenomenon. It also helps them understand that you are trying to empathize with them, unlike others who will shut them down. You can ask your child if he wants to be left alone without being disturbed.

Also, as a parent, the sight of your child crying might be quite uncomfortable for you and may make you feel agitated. If this isn't the case, you may ask them to go to their room to air their emotion or excuse them if you are the one in their room.

8. What is your problem?

Most of us say this phrase when we are highly stressed, not because we don't like the person we are saying it to or that the person indeed has a problem. It also shows that we were not patient enough to tolerate the behavior of the person. The truth about the condition of an ADHD child is that it is not their choice, and hence they don't have a problem. You are the one having issues with the way they are behaving. Your moral support and comforting emotional actions can go a long way to teach them to live a happy life.

Instead of saying this, you can just try to: let them be or excuse yourself from their presence. You can also take a deep breath to recollect your understanding and control your emotions. Most time, the best thing you do at that moment of inspiration is to give space, engage yourself in other activities, then call their attention to the behavior after a while. When you do this, you should let them know that you were quite sad about that behavior and you expected better from them. The child will be able to understand you at a time when his impulsivity has been put under check.

9. You can never change; you will always do what you want

As a parent, it is not good to say such words because it shows that you are already getting discouraged and frustrated by the child's behavior. These words show that you have concluded that they will get better. The child deserves your belief, and it is his right that you have faith in him and appreciates his effort at getting better. When you say they can never change, there are chances that such might be the outcome. And that only shows that you are undermining your effort. Try as much as possible to control yourself whenever you are about to say such statements filled with absolutes.

One certain thing is that your child will be bored of hearing such words. He would have heard similar statements from friends and schoolmates. You saying it only validates their comment. You need to show your child that you are different and that you still have hope in him that he will get better. If he as a child is down with regrets, the onus lies on you as a parent to give him the necessary courage.

10. Why can't you just stay in a place?

Such a statement is not out of place for a mother that is dealing with a child who is struggling with a complex of hyperactivity and impulsivity. It might even be a thing of surprise to see a child diagnosed with ADHD staying in a place for a long time. So, it is simply a waste of time to say such words since their body movement is just a natural response to their brain functions.

There are also some children who, when they are eager to say something, love jumping up or struggle to stay glued to a seat but move from one seat to another to say their mind. Some children may even forget what they are to say if they are forced to stay in a place. So, in essence, trying to force an ADHD child to be glued to a position might do more harm than good. His condition is such that he should be very active, so a forceful attempt at countering such functions may have a counterproductive effect on the brain and might result in more complications. You need to give him all the attention that he needs.

It might just be good to show attention and go along with what he is saying, but so also is calling his attention to some obstacles on his path so he might avoid them.

It might be so tiring and discouraging when exercising your parenting skills on an ADHD child, but it is not what you think that matters, but what should be done. You must focus on your effort and appreciate the little progress. It is also normal to get distracted sometimes because you are too engrossed in helping your child that you forget about helping yourself.

11. I understand your feeling. I get all tensed up as well.

These words may have been uttered so that your child may feel connected to you and understand that you too feel his emotions. But, if you are not diagnosed with ADHD, such a comment might just be too forward and may also sound like you are trying to undermine his challenges and the feelings he has been struggling with. The child may think about why he cannot get it right when you are getting it right despite having the same feelings. So, even though such words were uttered to show connectedness, it might cause a wide gap to grow between the two of you because he might feel you have the solutions to his problem but are unwilling to show it to him

Therefore, instead of saying this, you can say, "I truly don't understand how you are feeling, but I am here for you if you need any help." By saying this, you can establish the needed connection and at the same time create more options to help your child. The child needs all the connections, especially emotionally, socially, and physically that he can get. So, trying to deny him of such is like working against your plan for success as a parent. There is much at stake, so you can not allow a moment of pity to rob your child of the connection that he needs.

It is very necessary not to look down on the challenges faced by your child and to not be selfish in your approach. You need to understand the uniqueness and the peculiarities of your child in terms of his emotions, feelings, and behaviors. It will also be helpful to try to see things from their perspective and use that to plan your strategies for support.

Chapter 14:
Parenting Questions

As a parent, there might be many things going on in your mind and a lot of questions about your child's unusual behavior. You might be disturbed with the thoughts of whether your child has ADHD or not and have no idea where to start from; here are some questions that you might have with their answers given.

Question: ADHD, what does it mean?

Answer: ADHD is an abbreviation that stands for Attention-Deficit/Hyperactivity Disorder. It is a known chronic condition that mostly affects children. It affects the neurodevelopmental function of the children. The main feature of the disorder includes lack of attention, impaired impulse control, and hyperactivity.

Question: I have heard about ADD. Is it the same with ADHD?

Answer: In the past, it was called ADD, but because it was confusing to many, it was changed to ADHD. Now, all forms of attention deficit disorder, which is what ADD means, are to be called Attention-Deficit/Hyperactivity Disorder, officially whether the diagnosed individual is hyperactive or not.

However, to date, a lot of professionals and non-professionals alike still the terms ADD and ADHD interchangeably. Some use ADD whenever they want to refer to the old subtypes, while others just stick with ADD because it is shorter and easier to pronounce.

Question: What does this executive function mean?

Answer: This is the apex function of the brain that controls every other function. That is the reason why it is called the executive function. It is a function that executes other functions. It is the one responsible for consequential accountability and planning. This means that it allows individuals to be accountable for their actions and prepare for the consequences. It also makes them evaluate their actions, predicts the consequences, and makes necessary modifications if it is not going according to plan.

Question: How is ADHD diagnosed?

Answer: There is no single test to diagnose ADHD. Therefore, a comprehensive evaluation is necessary to establish a diagnosis, rule out other causes, and determine the presence or absence of co-existing conditions.

Question: Can I know about ADHD diagnosis?

Answer: There is yet to be a single way of testing for ADHD. There is no test kit yet. What is done is a detailed evaluation of observed and supplied information. This is to drive out irrelevant symptoms, organize the relevant ones, identify the presence of another condition and come to a conclusion.

Such a process consumes time and effort. It involves a critical assessment of the academic, social and emotional skills as well as the level of development.

Question: Which specialist can help with diagnosis and treatment?

Answer: It is very important to consult qualified, registered, licensed, and experienced professionals. For the diagnosis of ADHD, different professionals can do so; these include psychiatrists, psychologists, social workers, nurse practitioners, licensed counselors, and more.

Question: Is there any relationship between ADHD and Obesity?

Answer: Among those with ADHD, the adult population is the one most concerned with their body weight. This, most of the time, does not concern those without the condition. A research carried out by the National Institute of Mental Health discovered that adults without ADHD have a reduced tendency of being overweight and obese compared to those with ADHD.

It was also discovered that the same trend goes for the children population. But, the input of quality management for ADHD is also a major determining factor. Reports have shown that ADHD children who do not have medications included in their management plan were one-half of the time more likely to get too much weight than those children who do have medication as part of their plan.

Question: Are there other conditions that occur with ADHD?

Answer: It has been shown that there is always a coexisting condition among more than half of individuals with ADHD. It is the over-demanding symptoms of ADHD such as inattention, hyperactivity, and impulsivity that overclouds the presence of this condition.

However, as ADHD can become dangerous if left untreated, so are these other co-existing conditions if left untreated. Different disorders can occur with ADHD, but certain disorders have been discovered to occur more frequently than others. Those that frequently occur than others include learning disorders, sleep disorders, substance abuse, anxiety, tics, or Tourette syndrome.

Question: In what way is ADHD treated?

Answer: To treat ADHD, there are various interventions such as medical, behavioral, psychological, and educational interventions. This combination approach to managing ADHD is influenced by the age of those with ADHD and may include: medication, counseling, skills training, behavioral therapy, parental training, and more.

Question: Is there anything I should know about how the medication is to be carried?

Answer: You should carry your ADHD medication in a marked container. Officers of law enforcement agencies are very wary of the possible occurrence of drug misuse or abuse, especially among young adults and adolescents. In case you were stopped by the police for violating the traffic laws or for misconduct and you were found with an unlabeled container, you put yourself at risk of being suspected as a drug abuser.

Question: My 3-year-old boy is extremely playful and finds it difficult to sit down in a place or focus on anything for long. His teacher at the daycare thinks he might be battling ADHD. Is this true? And can a toddler come up with ADHD?

Answer:

Well, this question is quite tricky. This is so because normally, toddlers often find it difficult to stay in a place and get distracted easily. They can't just stay in a place. They are very impatient and are quite messy. They don't care about the importance of focusing. They tend to jump from one play to another. Taking a cue from all these, it is easy to mistaken toddlers being their normal self for symptoms of ADHD.

This does not in any way imply that toddlers do not have ADHD. Some children are so severely active and very impulsive that it almost becomes unbearable and calls for immediate concern. At this stage, their playfulness and impulsivity start to affect their academic performance and social relationships.

So, it boils down to how severe their impulsive behavior is. A normal toddler is naturally active, but when ADHD is present, the activity level becomes very elevated, and they are now constantly talking and unable to control themselves. Now, unlike before, they will have more trouble sitting down for long, unable to initiate sleep and constantly wake up at night, stay long before they could sleep again. And quite different from a normal child will find it difficult to interact with others.

For a child who is of the age of 4 and older, there are prescribed guidelines that should be followed if the child shows any of the symptoms of ADHD. The American Academy of Pediatrics recommends that the child should be taken for ADHD evaluation.

There are still no guidelines for those younger, but some research has discovered that in the United States, evaluation can be carried out for toddlers.

Though it might be true that toddlers can be diagnosed with ADHD, other possible causes responsible for the manifesting symptoms must be duly considered. It should also be noted that children who have a delay with their developmental maturity may behave like someone younger.

In case you have anything to report about how your toddler is behaving, you can consult your health care practitioner. The recommended course is to do a physical and psychological examination, thereafter comprehensive assessment before proper diagnosing is carried out.

This is done to exclude other conditions that also have similar symptoms.

If you are seriously concerned that something might be wrong with your child, having taken critical considerations of the nature and patterns of his behavior, it is advised you go for the necessary consultations very early. You should access help early so that your child will get the help he needs before starting school.

Question: I heard that ADHD is somehow connected to Autism. Is this true?

Answer: ADHD and Autism are indeed connected in different ways. It should be stated that ADHD is quite different from Autism spectrum disorder, but have some of their symptoms being the same.

There has been a change in the way experts view the relationship between ADHD and autism. According to the Diagnostic and Statistical Manual of Mental Disorders, fourth edition (DSM-IV), a person can not develop both autism and ADHD, but the recent version, which is the fifth edition, has allowed the diagnosis of both conditions in the same person.

Now, to talk about the different symptoms of ADHD and Autism and where overlapping could take place, let's look at these two examples.

Difficulty with attention: Children with autism often battle with lack of attention for different reasons. One of the reasons is that having difficulty processing language may make it look like they are not attentive. Meanwhile, what happens is that they do not understand the directives that were given.

Difficulty socializing: Children with ADHD often have issues with interacting with others. It is either they try all they can to avoid interaction, or they are too hyperactive and encroaches into another person's personal space.

This is the reason why, most times, some children are misdiagnosed because the symptoms are overlapping. If you are troubled that your child is probably misdiagnosed, you can contact your physician. It is normal for physicians to deal with this kind of problem, so don't be scared; just make the call or visit as soon as possible.

Also, as it has been stated earlier, the presence of one of these conditions makes the child susceptible to the development of the other one. This is the case with most developmental conditions. There is often an underlying condition. As an example, it is expected for a kid who has issues with processing language to develop a learning disorder.

This is more of the reason why every aspect of the developmental functions of the child must be evaluated. These aspects include his mood, motor skills, social skills, attention, and behavior, etc. It is expected that you will get a comprehensive evaluation that will deal with all these areas when you visit a licensed professional.

It has also been discovered well that ADHD and autism have a genetic relationship. The chance is very high for someone who has had to have a close member of his extended family also having autism or other disorders that affect the development

This connection between the cause and symptoms of ADHD and autism can also be extended to their methods of management. This means that a method of management that works for one can also be for the other one. As an example, children who are diagnosed with both conditions are helped when they are subjected to home rules.

However, there is a big difference in the kind of treatment regimen that is prescribed for each of them. The treatment type recommended for autism is directed to help manage problems with communication and also help lower the level of repeating behaviors which is the main feature of the presence of autism.

While treatment for ADHD is directed at helping with controlling impulses and increasing attention. Medications are helpful most times but may do little or nothing for those with ADHD.

Most times, it will have been easy if the two conditions can be well separated as management will be much easier. But this is not the case in reality. A good understanding of both conditions is the first step to take in understanding their connective complications.

Question: My son was diagnosed with ADHD. He is now 9 years old and is still bedwetting at times. I will like to know if there is any relationship between bedwetting and ADHD?

Answer: There is a connection, yes. This is because it has been discovered that children with ADHD bed-wet three times as often as those who are not. This is often very challenging for both the child and the parent

It is still yet uncertain as to the reason why ADHD children are facing this issue which is also medically known as nocturnal enuresis. The view of some researchers is that this is happening simply because both conditions are caused by issues with the child's nervous development.

Another reason is that it may be because ADHD children often find it difficult to control their body impulses. Because of the high level of brain activity, they might be unsure of when their bladder gets full and where they are. This may be why they let out their urine without thinking about the consequences.

Naturally, nocturnal enuresis does resolve on its own. As these children mature, they tend to sleep and wake up with a dry bed because their body is now mature enough to:

1. Secrete enough of a substance called antidiuretic hormone, which helps to concentrate the urine.

2. Matures the bladder to accommodate more urine at night.

3. More aware of their bladder filling up during the night to wake up and empty it.

These three functions must be developed to increase the chances of waking up dry in the morning.

For kids with ADHD, that development may be slower or come later. But eventually, most kids with ADHD catch up to their peers, and the bedwetting stops.

Still, it's always a good idea to talk with your child's doctor if you have any concerns. Sometimes bedwetting can be a sign of other medical issues. (That's more often the case if it starts suddenly or if a child is also having accidents during the day.)

Here are some of the things you can help your child with

At the top of the list, you must discourage them from drinking any fluid for an hour prior to sleeping and to always ensure they visit the gents just before sleeping. You can also make use of an alarm that will help the child get up just before bedwetting at night.

1. It has also been discovered that both the parent and the child are impatient for this to get better along the way. If you are in the same category as these, it's better that you consult your physician about medications that will be helpful for stopping bedwetting.

2. These medications will only be used for specific purposes, such as when the child is sleeping over at other houses or in camps

3. Though it is true that wetting the bed is not a lifelong menace, it's normal for a parent to be anxious about it. However, a parent's reaction to the situation goes a long way in affecting the child's confidence.

4. Having a good knowledge about the various issues that affect development with those with ADHD will further help to make understanding and supporting the child a lot easier. One thing you should be aware of is that anxiety is not good for the issue. It may further compound the problem.

Question: My 7-year-old daughter had been battling with motor tics since she was 5. Recently, she was diagnosed with ADHD. Is there any connection between tics and ADHD? And will the use of medications for ADHD make the tic worse?

Answer: ADHD and tics are quite related. It has been reported that about 50 percent of those who are diagnosed with chronic tics also have ADHD. At the same time, a quarter of children with ADHD are seen with chronic tics.

To say a child has a tic, he must have been having spontaneous and hard to control repetitive movements or the incessant making of sounds. It may be repeated episodes of eye movement or repeated shaking of the head. This is known as motor tics. Vocal tics, on the other hand, are repeated episodes of making sounds such as sneezing, coughing or sniffing, etc.

Most tics do happen on and off and take different forms over time. Over time, most children with these tics eventually grow out of it. However, some tics are stubborn and often persist.

As of now, what is known is that stimulant medications may be responsible for making tics manifestations worse. But there are other contradictions to this as well. One of them is that the manifestations of tics are independent of ADHD medication use. Also, it is yet to be proven that there is any tangible connection between the use of these drugs and tics manifestation.

There was an analysis of findings that was carried out about this problem at Yale University as far back as 2015. The research takes a critical look at a group of studies that studied over 2000 children with ADHD and tics. It was found out that there is nothing to support the claim that ADHD medication use can cause or worsen tics.

However, one cannot rely on this as it is data collected from groups. There are still some children with ADHD who are susceptible to tics whose tics manifestations may worsen when a stimulant medication is taken.

Also, some ADHD medications are non-stimulating, and that seems to help with tics. Though these medications are not effective for treating

ADHD themselves, they are complemented by other stimulant medications.

A child with ADHD and tics can still make use of stimulant medications safely. No child is the same, so what works for one may not work for the other child. There might be a need for some modifications. It is good to contact your physician and discuss your fears.

Question: I am seriously disturbed about my 7-year old child. I think she might have been misdiagnosed with ADHD. How can I be sure, and what can I do now?

Answer: First of all, there is a need to understand your emotions. How do you know if your child had the wrong diagnosis? Are you basing your judgment on your instincts, or are you basing it based on the information you got from someone?

But, if you are troubled and doubting your child's diagnosis as a parent, the very first step to take is to get through to the physician who made the diagnosis in the first place. There is nothing wrong with making more inquiries and getting more information from the person.

There are two main areas you should be interested in when you are making your inquiry. First is the information that was evaluated before making the diagnosis, and the second is how well your child has been responding to management.

When asking your questions and conversing about what led up to the final diagnosis, you should remember to ask the physician:

If the physician was aware of the important information about the developmental milestones of your child. The details of the progress or dysfunction in behavior and emotional regulation are critical for making the right diagnosis.

If he demanded that all those involved in taking care of your child and yourself fill out some measuring tools. This is important for the crucial collection of quantifiable data for diagnosis.

For a proper diagnosis to be done and ADHD diagnosed, some symptoms of ADHD must be present for at least six months. Also, these symptoms must have impaired your child's ability to function in multiple settings. As an example, your child must have been having issues that you can bear witness to at home and also report some unruly behaviors at school.

As far as ADHD symptoms are concerned, there are some other questions you should ask the physician about, like if he was sure that he could observe the symptoms and they are not something else. This is because other conditions can occur with ADHD and can also occur alone and be misjudged because they share the same symptoms with ADHD.

For example, ADHD isn't the only condition with symptoms of reduced attention. The cause for this symptom and their treatment might be quite different.

Highlighted below are some factors that could still affect the accuracy of the diagnosis given to your child:

- Sleep
- Anxiety
- Depression
- Learning differences
- Trauma or chronic stress
- Immaturity

To be clear, ADHD diagnosis is made worldwide, and even though the above-highlighted factors can influence diagnosis, they can also occur together with the diagnosis. ADHD and other conditions do exist together.

Different things can influence making an effective diagnosis of ADHD. It is not something that can be done on an appointment or within fifteen minutes. It also takes time to get the right management method.

Maybe you are thinking because the management is not working for your child, and it could be that the right treatment is being used for the wrong diagnosis. This might be true, and it may also be that the management is yet to be given the time it needs to be effective or that you were given the wrong dosage of ADHD medications. These are some of the things that must be considered.

If you have discussed all these deeply and critically with the physician who made the diagnosis and you are still not convinced, there is nothing wrong with going for a second opinion.

You can go to another physician and get a comprehensive evaluation of all the areas earlier mentioned. No matter the doubt, the best cure is to get more information, and this can be gotten from professionals and consultants. You can also try your child's teachers; they stay longer with your child than you.

Chapter 15:
How to Eliminate ADHD symptoms in children

The preceding chapter successfully expatiated how people can easily recognize ADHD symptoms in children by unveiling some of these common symptoms, including a low level of attention and a high level of distraction, hyperactivity, impulsiveness, and attention-demanding. From a clearer angle, these symptoms can further be elaborated and discussed in other simple terms:

- **Forgetfulness**: Forgetfulness is one of the common symptoms you may expect from a child with ADHD. For instance, a child with ADHD may forget to do a task given after just a few minutes of hearing it. This situation may look atypical because the child's action will be as if you've never talked about the task.

- **Spacy**: You can easily identify a child battling attention deficit hyperactivity disorder as they may sometimes be apathetic or spacey.

- **Inattentiveness**: Inability to pay proper attention to things is a common challenge that a child with ADHD may tend to experience. They often find it problematic to be attentive.

- **Problem with follow-through**: Well, the essence of starting a project is to see it get done to the end. This may not apply to a child with ADHD. They may have problems with the continuance or completion of a project. This implies that they may fail to follow instructions and be unable to finish given projects.

- **Distraction**: When you talk of a child with ADHD, you may want to talk about how they can usually be distracted. Children with ADHD are often easily distracted.

- **Loss of necessary things**: A child with ADHD that is given a task to handle or engages in a specific activity may lose things important for the task or activity.

- **Poor focus**: Undoubtedly, when your ability to pay proper attention to things is affected, you will definitely have challenges with being focused. For children with ADHD, this is a major challenge. They consistently appear not to be paying the required attention to what people tell them or what's happening at the moment.

- **Carelessness**: Carelessness may be a challenge the parents of a child with ADHD may want to deal with. Children with ADHD usually have problems paying attention to details which may result in them making careless mistakes.

- **Problem with listening to people**: Children with ADHD may usually not listen when they are being spoken to.

- **Avoidance of mental effort**: Children with ADHD often detest tasks that need sustained mental effort. This makes them avoid or feel reluctant to engage in them.

- **Problem with being organized**: Children with ADHD usually have a challenge with organizing tasks and activities.

- **Frequent bursts of energy**: Children with ADHD often have their energy burst. They may be observed to be overly active relative to where they find themselves— they often bounce off the walls.

- **Interruption**: Children with ADHD are often known for interrupting activities and people at home or in class.
- **Constant fidgeting**: Children with ADHD have problems with sitting still. They can't just do it. They characteristically fidget almost constantly.

With the recognition of some of the common ADHD symptoms that can be found in a child with ADHD, it's very important to discuss how to eliminate them. There are several reasons why you can't ignore these symptoms as parents that really care about their children living well. When children have ADHD, they often find it difficult to embrace the joy in life because they are not fully present. Their behaviors often make it difficult for them to interact in a protective, cooperative, and fulfilling manner with those around them. Their education is also affected by this, which may have negative implications on their future career possibilities.

Moreover, in relationships, these behaviors create more challenges for them than most people without ADHD. With the discomfort you can experience as parents of a child showing the symptoms of ADHD, which may sometimes get on your nerves, you may want to seek the way out. Nonetheless, it's very important to know that offering your child a pill each day may not be the best treatment option to go for.

No matter what you aim to do to eliminate your child's condition, you must know that your action begins at home. Every parent can easily influence their child's treatment. There are lots of things you can get to do as parents. Some of these may include ensuring they get plenty of exercise, giving them a healthy diet, and making other helpful daily choices.

To eliminate the symptoms of ADHD, you may want to consider the following:

1. **Exercise**. The power of exercise has a lot to offer as far as positively transforming the state of your child's health to live a better life. As an effective method, exercise is great, and it assists in boosting the levels of serotonin, dopamine, and norepinephrine in the brain. Consequently, it helps such a child to focus and pay proper attention. The good news is you don't need anyone to prescribe exercise for you, and it has no side effects. Some of the activities that have to with body movements and can help your kids that have ADHD include martial arts, gymnastics, skateboarding, and dance. You may want to engage them in team sports as they may find the situation interesting if a social element is employed.

2. **Good sleep:** Regular good sleep can greatly improve a child's condition. Despite how important quality sleep is in eliminating ADHD symptoms, some children have challenges sleeping at night. This problem may be because of medications (stimulants) or not. So, if your children experience this difficulty sleeping, you can help by:

    • Setting a regular bedtime which must be enforced

    • Looking for a way (perhaps a sound of a fan or a machine) to prevent your child from being kept up by background noise if that's the cause of the problem.

- Turning off all electronics (such as video games, computers, iPhone, or TV) at least one hour before bed.

- Embracing good nutrition— Good nutrition plan (regular snacks or meals no more than three hours apart) can help make steady the blood sugar of your child, minimize irritability, and support focus and concentration. Adding little protein and complex carbohydrates at every meal or snack can help your child become more alert as hyperactivity decreases. Ensure that your child's iron, zinc, and magnesium levels are okay as they help deal with ADHD symptoms. Besides, adding more omega-3 fatty acids to their diet can help reduce impulsivity and hyperactivity and enhance their concentration

- Limiting physical activity in the evening.

3. **Seek professional assistance**: Even if there are several ways you can deal with ADHD symptoms in a child, there are times you may need to seek professional help on your journey to giving such a child a great life. Numerous ADHD specialists can assist you with the right methods to help your child. You're advised to consult different specialists since ADHD can be tackled best by combining different strategies and treatments.

To get a specialist, you can get in touch with your primary care provider, local hospitals, child's pediatrician, or clinics. You may also want to access other sources to get provider references, including officials at your child's school, your insurance company, or a local parent support group.

Some specialists and what they do

o **Educational specialists**: Educational specialists help by advising families about assistive technology, helping children obtain accommodations from school, and teaching techniques for succeeding in school

o **Cognitive-behavioral therapists**: Cognitive-behavioral therapists help by establishing concrete goals for behavior and achievement, assisting families and teachers in maintaining rewards and consequences, and setting up behavioral modification programs at school, work, and home.

o **Psychologists**: Psychologists help those with ADHD explore their feelings, diagnose ADHD, and provide talk therapy.

o **Child and adolescent psychiatrists**: Child and adolescent psychiatrists help diagnose ADHD and prescribe medications.

4. **Use behavioral therapy (for ADHD):** Behavioral therapy or behavioral modification is a great way to help deal with the symptoms of ADHD in children. It can be used along with stimulants for children with ADHD. In behavioral therapy, desired behaviors are reinforced via rewards and praise, and problem behaviors are reduced by setting limits and consequences. A good example of this may be when a teacher intervenes by rewarding a child with ADHD for making little

effort by raising a hand before speaking in class, disregarding the fact that such a child speaks suddenly without thinking. The theory behind behavioral therapy is that full new behavior can be encouraged by rewarding the struggle toward change.

Furthermore, there are three basic principles to any approach of behavior therapy, as claimed by the American Academy of Pediatrics. The following may be helpful:

o **Try to set specific goals for your child**: You can help a child with ADHD set clear goals such as sharing toys with friends or staying focused on homework.

o **Try to provide rewards and consequences:** Everyone (especially kids) loves to be rewarded. Provide children with ADHD with positive reinforcement when they show the desired behavior. You may also need to offer a consequence (punishment or unwanted result) as it demands when they cannot meet a goal.

o **Try to keep using the rewards and consequences:** Your child's behavior can be shaped in a positive way when you consistently use rewards and consequences for a long time.

There is a customized behavioral modification program you can set up for your children with ADHD. You can seek the assistance of a behavioral specialist (such as a cognitive-behavioral therapist). With the help of a cognitive-behavioral therapist, practical solutions will be given to your child's day-by-day issues by setting up a behavioral modification program of rewards and consequences for such a child at home and school and assist you in shaping the child's behavior.

You must know that behavioral therapy does require patience. Parents sometimes may feel discouraged thinking that the method they engage in is not working as expected. Nevertheless, with behavioral treatment, they will see improvement in the symptoms of ADHD if they don't relent.

5. **Engage in social skills training:** Social skills training is another awesome approach to help a child with ADHD. Since children with attention deficit hyperactivity disorder usually struggle with low self-esteem and have difficulty with simple social interactions, social skills training can be a great way to deal with such conditions. Social skills training normally takes place in an organized group setting. It's anchored by a therapist who demonstrates appropriate behaviors and then asks the children to practice and repeat them. The social skills group aims at teaching kids how to read people's reactions and those behaviors that are acceptable.

Chapter 16:
20 Errors to Avoid While Raising an ADHD Child

Attention deficit hyperactivity disorder can sometimes make everyday tasks frustrating for parents of a child that has it. These parents can easily explain the trouble they have to go through, from getting such a child in bed at night to getting him out the door in the morning. It's undoubtedly like a daily tug of war nurturing a child diagnosed with ADHD.

In the attempt to deal with their child's situation, they will look to every possible place for help. They may read books and listen to behavioral experts speak on the tips of parenting for a child with ADHD, but the condition persists with no signal of any improvement. You must know that ADHD has a lot to do with a " brain difference." The way the brain of your child works is different from the way the brain of most of his peers (about 95%) works. So, for your child, adopting " one size fits all" parenting strategies may fail to work.

There may be times you feel like hauling objects after a long day attending to the needs of your child with ADHD. This is experienced by a lot of people. So, don't see yourself as the only person in the whole world facing such a challenge. There are lots of parents of children with

ADHD that consistently feel dejected and frustrated from daily push-back and yelling.

There are times you will think that every of your effort to get your child to do a specific task fails. But you should know that it's not all about them all the time. It is also very much about you. Your children need you when it comes to learning important executive functioning skills such as planning, organization, self-regulation, and prioritizing. And for them to realize all these, you have to be patient with them even during periods when their condition is becoming unbearable for you— you must hang in there.

Try to manage yourself if you intend to make headway in dealing with your child's condition. You may want to work on your empathy; work with them to provide solutions; make it known to them that you see how they are trying, and then encourage their efforts and see if there is any progress.

There are things every parent must know while helping their children get over their condition. As a parent, you should know that even merely by listening to the voice of your child with ADHD, there can be an improvement in success and cooperation. To do things differently and get incredible positive results, you may want to know about the parenting strategies which have been proven to be effective over time to be of great help to hundreds of families to reduce the stress they tend to experience in their journey to deal with Attention Deficit Hypersensitivity Disorder, to build more intimate relationships, and improve every day living. These parenting strategies include self-control, compassion, collaboration, consistency, and celebration. As parents, when these strategies are learned and practiced, you will realize how easy it is to be the great parent that your children need.

Nonetheless, there are errors some parents do make while raising a child with ADHD. These errors should be avoided. Some of these errors are explained as follows:

1. **Losing your temper:** Although it may be a natural reaction when you get upset, especially when you're frustrated, you should try as much as possible to control yourself when you begin to find your child's kicking, screaming, or hitting uncomfortably. Getting upset will only add fuel to the fire. Interestingly, every adult can control their emotions since their mature thinking brain is right at the pre-frontal lobes. But children and teens battling with ADHD need help from their parents to learn how to control their emotions because their pre-frontal lobes will not finish maturing until they are 25 or later.

   A parent can be of great assistance to their children practicing self-control. You should learn how to manage your feelings first, then you're ready to act properly and teach your child how to do the same. You should know that it's not that you will free from losing your temper, but you will be in charge of it by bringing yourself back when you're about to rile up.

2. **Misunderstanding your child's experience as a young person living with ADHD**: There is a higher probability that you will forget to notice that your child is giving everything the best it requires due to your struggle to attend to some other significant issues that need to be dealt with. There may be some things attached to why your child is exhibiting some behavior at a certain point in time. It could be that such a child is trying to get some things done or struggling with organization and not that such a child intends to create chaos. So, you may want to involve empathy in this area. Try to be compassionate and hope that your child will change while trying your best to make things better. You need to give them more time to develop their daily executive functioning skills.

3. **Excluding your child from participating in creating solutions to daily problems:** Not getting your child involved when it comes to creating solutions to everyday problems is one of the mistakes some parents do make. As other children have been gifted with ideas, kids with ADHD have their own unique ideas about things that are not working and things that could be better. You should offer the chance to make their input. Employ collaboration and let your child with ADHD give opinions to address areas of problems instead of imposing rules on them. Collaboration simply implies working together with your child to provide solutions to everyday challenges. Let them see you not as an opponent but as an ally.

4. **Threatening consequences or making plans that you won't be able to follow or do:** it's a big mistake not to follow them or go as planned. You should know that children with ADHD thrive on predictability and routine in spite of their protests. It's confusing when a parent finds it difficult to improvise a spontaneous punishment or follow a behavioral plan. You should mean what you say. Be consistent and when you fail to be, ensure you move on. You are not perfect, but ensure that you stay as steady as possible. Not giving your child with ADHD consequences that you can't support, remember, or enforce is what is called consistent parenting. You should let them learn that actions have consequences.

5. **Being too focused on the outcome and ignoring their efforts along the way:** It's a mistake to be expecting immediate changes in the behavior of a child with ADHD when you engage in a behavioral plan or give feedback. The goal of helping such a child become responsible and productive later on in life may sometimes overshadow your efforts. Your child may give up if the feedback on how such a child should do things better becomes inordinate. Well, it's great to focus on the outcome, but when it's too much, your child may lose momentum and motivation.

    To help your children effectively, you need to acknowledge their progress with celebration. Try to show that you notice their efforts and that you're very pleased with what they do.

6. **Sweating the small stuff:** Being too rigid with a child with ADHD is one of the mistakes many parents do make. You should be flexible with the task you assigned to them. Understand that

the child is still in the learning process, so every step such a child takes counts. You should be ready to make compromises with such a child.

7. **Getting overwhelmed and lashing out**: Virtually every parent of children with ADHD tends to experience discomfort at a certain time. But letting overwhelmed by such a situation is a mistake you can make. You should know that your child's behavior is from a disorder. Treat such a condition as a disability when you start to feel frustrated and angry. Know that your child can't become normal or snap out of the condition overnight.

8. **Being negative**: This is one of the greatest errors you can make while parenting a child with ADHD. You may be tempted to show a negative reaction when stressed, but you should know that it won't always be like that. Ensure you take things at a time each day and keep things in perspective.

9. **Letting your child or the disorder take control**: It's a mistake when you allow your child or the disorder to take from you the control. You're the parent, and ensure you persistently establish your rules for acceptable and unacceptable behavior. You don't want to be intimidated or bullied by the behavior of your child. Besides, you need to be nurturing and patient.

10. **Setting expectations out of scale for a child with a developmental disorder:** For every child, there are certain skills they possess at some specific levels of development. Around five months of age, babies are expected to roll over; by 9 months, they should become socially interactive with caregivers; and by age 2, they should be using 2-word phrases.

Normally, a child should begin to show more independence by age 5 in a very successful way. Their interest is expected to grow by the time they become adolescents in their future and planning it.

Nevertheless, if your children have ADHD, you should know that they are likely to be 2 to 3 years behind the calendar age developmentally. This also means that they fall 2 to 3 years behind their peers with emotional, social, and cognitive skills. It's important to adjust the standard you set for your children— this is to ensure that both of you end up successful. Put the following questions in mind when you intend to consider expectations for your children and let your answers guide you: At what age are they functional? What is my child's developmental age? What opportunities can I offer that my child can meet expectations and succeed in? What are appropriate expectations for a child that is my child's developmental age?

11. **Assuming that your children simply don't care to do well**: From a considerable perspective, it's claimed that children do well if they can. Here, the ability should be duly noted. If you discover that your kids are not doing well in a specific area, perhaps in school, you should know that it's that they decide not to care about it, or don't care to do it well, but it's because they are unable to get it done as expected as a result of their environment, disability, or lagging skills at the moment. The mistake is to assume that they don't just care to do well. Try to know the reason for their behavior and work to deal with or alleviate the reason. Doing this will help your

children do better. Instead of assuming that your children don't care about doing well, try to assume that your children care about doing well and care what adults and peers think of them. Seeing them not doing well, try to know why and ensure that you effectively address it. This will give honor to the personal truth of the child and open the path of success.

12. **Pushing your children to live your idea of childhood, and participate in your idea of what children of their age ought to be like, be interested in, and do excel at**: It's absolutely a mistake to push your kid to reenact life during your school days. Everyone most times feels nostalgic about some activities and events in their childhood. These may include team sports, summer camp, family movie nights, spending summers outside and active with your buddies, annual 4th of July fireworks, and so on. Doing this may have become a tradition mandated by culture for kids, but ensure you avoid this in the lives of children with ADHD.

You must know that what you experience during your childhood days for your own generation is likely to be different from what your children with ADHD can engage in successfully or intend to participate in. Try to concede with what your child has an interest in and not what you think they should have to get themselves involved in. When you push your children to do what you want them to do or what you think they should experience, what you do is setting expectations that are not realistic, not embracing who they are, and damaging their self-esteem.

13. **Dismissing your children's feelings**: Before you mistake dismissing your children's feelings as too babyish, intense, or not factual, you may want to remind yourself of their developmental age. At age 9, most children begin to show good emotional regulation skills. Nonetheless, for kids with ADHD, even though they are 9, with a developmental disorder, they are more like 6. So, for them, they are not likely to regulate their emotions as well as their peers. Their emotional reactions could easily be triggered in an inappropriate way for their calendar age.

Instead of dismissing your children's feelings because you think they aren't age-appropriate or too intense, you can try to show empathy and acknowledge the way things feel to them at present.

14. **Believing that a child with ADHD can simply wish their symptoms away**: You should understand that kids with ADHD battle with difficulties that are brain-based and will not disappear just because such kids wish them to. Children with ADHD are observed to do much better when they decide to work hard— if there is a deadline for them to meet, they work hard to make it possible. It's a mistake to assume that these children can get the work done simply because there is a deadline right in front of them, which makes them care more. The fact is that when these children have an impending due date to meet, their brain is activated by the late rush to meet the deadline. The activation of the brain may be in a way that compensates for some under-arousal the ADHD brain demonstrates, including

increased release of dopamine, increased neuron self-stimulation, and increase production of the Basal Ganglia.

There are other kinds of unconscious compensation, which include the use of caffeine or sugar to enhance the ability of the brain to focus and organize. Check this out; you can discover that the brain of a child is reacting to the threat in a way that makes work more doable. You should know that a late rush seldom normally results in top quality work, and also human brain does not work in a way that it can perform for a long time under stress. Besides, a viable strategy for college, school, or work success is the last-minute rush seldom. You can't make your kids wish their condition away. What you can do is to help treat it by adopting a program that can the children develop new insight, skills, and self-esteem.

15. **Not screening for visual and auditory problems (sensory processing challenges) that stimulate learning difficulties**: There is a possibility that may confuse sensory problems with ADHD since those with sensory problems can have symptoms similar to that of attention deficit hyperactivity disorder. This may include the production of poor attention and concentration, failure to complete assignments, and failure to stay on task. Dealing with sensory difficulties helps de-stigmatize emotional and academic struggles and can result in raised self-esteem and improved performance.

16. **Being ignorant of the cardinal rule of intelligence**: Smartness does not mean the ability to know how to do everything successfully. It's incorrect to assume that based on the fact that a child is capable of handling advanced

responsibilities or understand an advanced concept, so, such a child automatically knows the way to study, read, write, and address the mundane practicalities of life effectively.

17. **Overuse of punishment to motivate change and success:** According to research, punishment is an effective way to get someone to stop negative behavior. However, punishment will never be effective when it comes to getting such a person to do more of another behavior. Therefore, when you punish children for not doing their assignments m, it doesn't mean more assignments will be done. Punishment usually leads to a greater effort toward escaping being caught and consequently avoiding punishment. Besides, children with ADHD make mistakes so often that punishment will no longer mean a lot to them. If you want an increase of desired behaviors in your child, you will need to employ positive reinforcement of achievable goals and objectives that are communicated.

18. **Not acknowledging the negative messages they hear when you consistently praise their intelligence in lieu of their resiliency**: Children with ADHD may become trapped by being told that they are smart. Hearing this consistently will make them believe that: adults are expressing themselves truthfully, which may consequently make the children guilty of not using their gifts and become frustrated that they are unable to use these gifts when they want to or adults are not telling the truth, meaning that the children are dumb. You teach your children that success is from persevering through difficulty when you praise their resilience. Doing this

can also help inoculate them against stress and inform them that success is from behavior they can choose.

19. **Postponing parent self-care**: Parenting involves so many things. One of the essential things every parent must know is putting the needs of their children before theirs. It's a big mistake when parents are selfish by not prioritizing the needs of their children but attending to theirs first and deal with that of the children later.

20. **Focusing on the weaknesses of your children more than their strengths**: it's a mistake to concentrate on children's weaknesses more than their strengths— you shouldn't remind them constantly of their weaknesses. As parents, your job is to make sure that your children feel like they possess more strengths than weaknesses; that they have opportunities to boost their self-esteem and confidence; and that they feel they can have successes. Try to determine what your kids are good at, what they are passionate about, what they like doing, and offer them many opportunities in such areas.

Chapter 17:
10 Keys to parenting children with ADHD

The place of parenting can not be overemphasized as far as helping a child with attention deficit hyperactivity disorder. As parents, how you respond to your child's condition will decide how it will be: it can either be on the better side or the worse side.

There is no doubt in the fact that parenting a child diagnosed with ADHD can particularly be challenging. Some things can be very useful for you in relation to helping your kids with ADHD. Nevertheless, you should know that children are different from one another and what will work perfectly for one family may not work in the same way for another. The following keys are confirmed to be effective by experts who see them as strategies that have been of incredible help to a lot of families of kids with ADHD.

1. **Work with others as a team**: Working together with other individuals as a team is one strategy you can adopt. Those involved in the treatment of the child, such as parents, therapists, educators, tutors, and others, are expected to be on the same page as far as treatment plans and goals are concerned. They should be able to share information concerning how to care for the child to ensure that such a child gets every needed support. Try to take your child's teachers as allies and work hand-in-hand with them for desired outcomes both at home and in school.

2. **Embrace structure and predictability:** If you have a child with ADHD, you should know that they are deeply in need of clear definitions of expectations and routines. Interestingly, predictability is not only helpful for children with ADHD. It can also be of great assistance to adults suffering from ADHD. To help your child with the use and comprehension of schedules, you can make a daily schedule including time to do homework, get ready for school, play or free time, and bedtime. There are children (older ones) that can benefit from the use of timers, clocks, or charts to help in managing the day. If your children find this helpful, they can check items off the checklist as they are done.

3. **Define rules and expectations**: For parenting children with ADHD, you are expected 50 clearly define rules and expectations. When it comes to dealing well with ambiguity or changes in rules and expectations, children with ADHD are found wanting.

4. **Use positive feedback:** Everyone knows what the terms "positive" and "negative" connote when it comes to feedback. If you desire to help your children with ADHD deal with their challenges effectively, you will need to use more positive feedback when you talk with them. You are expected to be specific, concrete, and praise them for those awesome things they do or complete at the stated time and not consistently criticizing their behaviors which may be from the characteristic symptoms of ADHD. Instead of offering incentives or prizes that are costly, try to reward their positive behavior with rewards such as a special privilege or special time with you.

5. **Use appropriate consequences for negative behaviors**: Every parent must know that consequences may sometimes negatively affect children with ADHD. Normally, the consequences for children with ADHD shouldn't be based on something that occurs in the future but an immediate event. As far as other aspects of the schedule you have for your kids with ADHD are concerned, you must ensure that the consequences for their negative behavior are predictable and consistent.

6. **Be specific when giving instructions:** Specificity is very important when helping a child with ADHD. Focusing on one event or task at a time when instructing your kid may be very important. For younger kids, it can be helpful to break a task down into component steps. There are specific instructions and general instructions. Specific instructions are more helpful for children with ADHD.

7. **Tackle one thing at a time:** Don't make the mistake of trying to tackle all tasks at the same time. It's much better to focus on one or two problems when you decide to help your child get over several behavior challenges. Be strategic and set both short-term and long-term goals. For the short-term, it can be learning to control interruptions at the dinner table for 10 minutes at a time, and for the long-term, it can be putting an end to interrupting at the dinner table 90% of the time. Besides, you have to remember to use praise and rewards for achievements.

8. **Help to eliminate distractions and manage time**: It's very important to take some responsibilities seriously. One of these is offering needed help to older children or teens to establishing a homework routine that is without distraction.

You can employ the use of a timer to help your child with homework to focus on a specific subject for a given amount of time or to plan 10-minute breaks after each hour of homework. Also, it can be helpful to view long-term projects such as term papers and come up with an action plan for such projects, dividing them into manageable steps. Technology is taking charge in the present age, so don't be astonished when you discover that older children may be keenly interested in using mobile apps for time management.

9. **Model a healthy lifestyle:** Life generally demands a healthy lifestyle for good living. The best place your children can see how things should be ideally done is in you. So, you are expected to be a good role model to them. They look up to you, and you don't want to fail them. Ensure that you model the choices you would like to see them make regarding nutrition, diet, and exercise. With the right intake of a healthy diet and proper maintenance of normal weight, your children can face the demands of attention deficit hyperactivity disorder and even other life stressors.

10. **Value and embrace their uniqueness**: ADHD is suffered by many individuals, even the popular and highly accomplished people. Always let your kids know this and help them discover areas they can do well. Besides, ensure you show them your unconditional love for how unique they are.

Conclusion

According to what has already been discussed, the first place the persisting problems that a child battling with Attention-Deficit/Hyperactive Disorder (ADHD) is first recognized is usually in the school by teachers, school psychologist, and school counselors who then relay this information to the parent of the child and ask them to also observe some set of behaviors at home.

In other cases, especially in this modern world where the knowledge of ADHD has spread far and wide, parents of their volition without any special consultation start to observe their children and get suspicious when some of the behaviors of their children are going beyond what is considered normal for their peers.

It must also be emphasized again that, in either of the above cases, the determination of the potential reason for the unusual behaviors of your child can only be done through the right medical consultation.

Parents are advised to contact a health professional who has the necessary knowledge and experience about the possible ranges of physical, psychological, and developmental issues that can be found among children.

To help you in your quest to find what is happening to your child or what might be responsible for the unusual behavior that has been identified by significant others at school and by friends and families, you must seek medical advice. Many parents depend on hearsay and information given by other parents without proper consultation with professionals trained to do such.

A comprehensive evaluation that is critical and thorough is essential for proper and accurate diagnosing of your child's condition. It is only when an accurate diagnosis is made that the due management plan can be designed.

A child psychiatrist and a pediatrician are the health professionals likely to have the professional know-how about your child's problems.

Every medical doctor undergoes at least four years of medical training in medical school with a year of general medical training as a graduate in a clinical setting which is popularly known as internship. After this, they undergo additional training in a specialty of their choice, in this case, child psychiatry.

Here they will be under postgraduate training for two years in adult psychiatry and another two years in child psychiatry before they are registered and licensed as a specialist after passing the board exams.

Every psychiatrist, just like other physicians, is to progress in their learning by attending seminary and undergoing several courses. Also, they need to engage themselves in other academic-related activities to update their medical licenses. These licenses are reissued annually by the board of the specialty at certain prescribed periods.

Child psychiatrists are the ones in the best position to evaluate and manage children with ADHD. This is because they have undergone several training sessions, and they have been exposed to different sections of teaching regarding mental health disorder diagnosis and treatment, not just the ADHD, but all other childhood psychiatric disorders, which also includes the other conditions that do occur together with ADHD and those that might be mistaken for it.

The majority of child psychiatrists now believe that most of the disorders that are evaluated by them are being caused by genetic and biological factors and are at best treated with medications. A child psychiatrist is also equipped with life experiences of how to evaluate and treat problems of psychological and developmental basis that may develop or exist together with childhood ADHD. Also, the necessary and best treatment modalities for these disorders are well known to him.

A pediatrician can also manage ADHD and other problems that are related to childhood. He also likes a child psychiatrist who undergoes two years of clinical internship to learn about the medical disorders that do affect children and adolescents, which also involves some short time training in child psychiatry. There is another sub-specialist in the pediatric specialty known as the behavioral pediatrician. This specialist is trained to be able to manage behavioral challenges faced by children and is capable of managing the ADHD condition in children.

There are also many pediatricians and family physicians who manage several patients with ADHD. There are different reasons for this. One of them is that most parents who have a child with ADHD who were referred to go and see a child psychiatrist may not want to go with the belief that their child's condition is not so severe to the extent of seeing a psychiatrist.

They fear that accepting such a referral would mean that their child is much sicker than they had realized. Sometimes pediatricians or general physicians treat ADHD patients because they feel they can handle it themselves or because they feel there are no competent child psychiatrists in the community. Finally, there are simply too few child psychiatrists to treat the number of children in the community who require help.

There is a wide gap between the skill of a pediatrician and a family practitioner in the way they can handle the diagnosis, psychological management, and therapeutic assistance of those with ADHD. Some of them are not so versed in managing behavioral problems because it is not part of their training, while others can only treat medical cases and quickly refer the more complicated psychiatric problems to the child psychiatrists. There are others who do not acknowledge the complexity of children with ADHD and tend to deal with all the children the same way, which lessens the quality of management they can provide.

Finally, it is your duty as a parent to take care of your child and to get the best management for him as soon as possible. As you have already learned, getting your child evaluated as early as possible is one of the hallmarks of quality and better outcomes. There will be discouragement from naysayers, but you owe it to yourself and your child to be the best parent and try your possible best.

NOTES

NOTES